How to Slay a Dragon

How to Slay a Dragon
Building a New Russia After Putin

MIKHAIL KHODORKOVSKY

Translated by Stephen Dalziel

polity

First published in Russian as *КАК УБИТЬ ДРАКОНА? Пособие для начинающих революционеров* in 2022

Copyright © MBK Productions. Agreement via Wiedling Literary Agency

This English edition © Polity, 2023

The right of Mikhail Khodorkovsky to be identified as Author of this Work has been asserted in accordance with the UK Copyright, Designs and Patents Act 1988.

Polity Press
65 Bridge Street
Cambridge CB2 1UR, UK

Polity Press
111 River Street
Hoboken, NJ 07030, USA

ISBN-13: 978-1-5095-6105-6

A catalogue record for this book is available from the British Library.

Library of Congress Control Number: 2023937103

Typeset in 11 on 14pt Warnock Pro
by Cheshire Typesetting Ltd, Cuddington, Cheshire
Printed and bound in Great Britain by CPI Group (UK) Ltd, Croydon

The publisher has used its best endeavours to ensure that the URLs for external websites referred to in this book are correct and active at the time of going to press. However, the publisher has no responsibility for the websites and can make no guarantee that a site will remain live or that the content is or will remain appropriate.

Every effort has been made to trace all copyright holders, but if any have been overlooked the publisher will be pleased to include any necessary credits in any subsequent reprint or edition.

For further information on Polity, visit our website:
politybooks.com

Contents

Preface

It was Mark Zakharov's cult film, *To Slay a Dragon*, that gave me the title of this book. In that film, the archivist, in justifying his conformist views to his knight, said: 'The only way to get rid of someone else's dragon is to create a dragon of your own.' And that's exactly how we live: first of all, we tolerate for a long time being tormented and oppressed by somebody else's dragon (in reality, it's our own, but it's an old one), then we finally rid ourselves of it – and create a new dragon of our own. But after a while this one, too, gets old and we stop regarding it as 'ours'. I am absolutely convinced that this vicious circle of Russian history can be broken, and that Russia is fully capable of living with its own mind and its own conscience, and without dragons. But in order to do this, the young knights of the revolution must bear in mind that it's not enough simply to slay the old dragon, even though this in itself is no easy task; it is vital also not to end up bringing to power a new dragon, and one that may prove to be even worse than its predecessor. This book is about how this can be achieved in Russia.

As a country we're in a difficult situation. Society already understands that 'we cannot go on like this'; but at the same time, we're frightened that things will only get worse.

Everyone in power, besides the president, realizes that there isn't a good way out; but everyone still hopes that 'maybe it will all blow over'.

The opposition has an overwhelming desire to sweep away the regime; but has no concept of 'what then?'.

Because of this, I believe that the time has come to explain clearly to the people what we're proposing and what answers we're offering to life's key philosophical questions. People have the right to know what to expect if they stand alongside us, and particularly what the principles are for which it's worth giving up a quiet life and risking their freedom and the safety of those dear to them.

But there is one thing we can say for sure: the time for burying your head in the sand and for turning a blind eye to the most serious social issues – that time has gone.

'We don't care about politics, we're only concerned about people turning our yard into a dumping ground'; 'we don't care about politics, we're just against abuse of power'; 'we don't care about politics, we're just concerned about artistic freedom, corruption, free access to the internet' – yes, the time for such quaint doublespeak has gone. If you 'don't care about politics', then just stand on the sidelines and wait. Maybe the dragon will be in a good mood and will give you something out of the kindness of its heart; but given the way things are today it's more likely that it'll kick you down and take your last crumb.

But if, on the other hand, you really want to stand up for your rights and the rights of others, then that means getting involved in genuine politics. It means making choices, and it means confrontation, with all the risks that this brings.

I occupy a unique place among the ranks of the opposition (true, this doesn't exactly make me jump for joy). I have huge managerial experience, having worked in the government and at the head of a number of the country's largest companies, companies that were of strategic significance to the country, and that were linked to dozens of towns and villages that were devoted solely to these industries. But, despite all this, I am deprived of the opportunity to carry out practical organizational work on the ground.

When they kicked me out of the country, the authorities slammed the door shut behind me and turned the key, making it absolutely clear that, in the event of my returning, I would face the rest of my life in prison.

At the same time, I am one of the very few who has personal experience (we could say, 'fortunately, very few', for this experience comes with a high price) who has actually told Vladimir Putin to his face exactly what I think about corruption at the highest levels of government. And just a month after doing this, I faced criminal charges and ended up being locked up for more than ten years (six in a prison cell and four in labour camps). Added to which I staged four hunger strikes, including two when I refused to take even liquids; and I carried out all of them until my demands were met, and, in the case of three of them, as a sign of solidarity.

Ten years. That's almost as much as my friend Platon Lebedev. It's immeasurably less than my colleague Alexei Pichugin, who's still in jail. It's easier than the fate that befell another of my colleagues, the lawyer Vasily Alexanyan, who only a year after his release died from a disease for which he was refused treatment while in prison.

I have something to put before these authorities; some things that will be remembered and some things that must never be forgotten.

But this is exactly why I don't want to talk about the past; rather, I suggest that we think about the future.

I don't believe I have the right to choose between justice and mercy; to forgive or to refuse to forgive those whom I consider should be punished.

I certainly don't consider myself to be 'the bearer of the ultimate truth'.

Each one of us has his or her own experience, our own scores to settle and our own thoughts on the future. But by virtue of the way in which my mind works, I have decided not to talk in terms of how 'it wouldn't be bad if we were to change those who are in power', but rather to discuss a practical plan of action as to what to do 'after Putin'.

From the way in which I think of time (and I look on time differently after the period I spent in prison), I believe that this regime does not have much of it left: no more than five or ten years. How it will end, I don't know. Probably together with Putin. After all that has happened in Ukraine, I find it very difficult to imagine that he will step down of his own choice and live out however much time God grants him on some paradise island somewhere. He simply won't be allowed to do that.

One way or another, this regime will meet its end. When it does, there will be so much that will have to be put right. And it has to be done quickly. It would be wonderful if, when this moment arrives, society has already decided who we are and where we're heading, in which direction the road is leading in this rapidly changing world . . .

Introduction: My Path into Politics and What I Hope to Achieve

Politics was never important for me in and of itself. Before I found myself locked up, I was involved in politics only inasmuch as I needed it for business; in other words, simply to achieve those economic goals that were my priority at the time. Then came prison. Prison is hardly the optimum place to discuss politics; but it's a good place to receive a political education. And this was what I earnestly strove to achieve when I wasn't occupied with the other tasks that are put upon you when you're in jail.

At the very end of 2013, Putin took the decision to release me. Even though, as they say, 'hope springs eternal', I considered the likelihood of such an outcome to my ten years of incarceration as highly improbable. To this day I genuinely have no idea what guided Putin's thinking. No doubt there were a number of different reasons. There was the forthcoming Winter Olympics in Sochi, which he knew had to pass off in exemplary fashion. Then there was the personal request from the German Chancellor Angela Merkel, which he calculated might lead to some sort of reciprocal concession. And, of course, there was the human emotion of compassion for my dying mother, for whom this would be the last chance to see me.

I was aware of all of these reasons and weighed them up while rapid preparations were being made for my expulsion from Russia. I understood, too, that without Putin's goodwill and wish for this to happen, I would never be set free; and also, that his decision upset a lot of people in his circle. Therefore, even though I honestly warned the FSB [Federal Security Service] officer who came to collect me that I did not intend to hide myself away from people and keep silent, I had absolutely no intention of becoming involved in politics simply to seek personal revenge. As far as I was concerned, my account was settled in my personal relationship with Putin: he had sent me down, thus depriving me and my family of ten years of my life; yet he had also saved my life. Looking back on matters now, it's perfectly clear that, had he not acted as he did then, I would have been confined behind bars to the end of my days.

So when I said after my release that I didn't intend to get involved in politics, I was completely sincere. I never had any desire to be involved in politics just to prove something to Putin, and that's still the case. Paradoxically, our personal relationship worked out in such a way that I even owe him something. He could have killed me, but he didn't. He could have left me to rot in jail, but he didn't. I haven't forgotten this. I planned to engage in targeted human rights and educational activities. It seemed to me that there was sufficient scope to employ my talents and my experience in these fields; and my money could also be very useful. But the more I became involved, the more intensely politics infiltrated into everything I touched. What had happened? What was it that convinced me to turn away from my initial firm resolve not to return to the world of politics?

In order to answer that question, I have to explain what I understand by 'political activity', and what my motivation is to engage in it. In the exact and only possible sense of the word, politics is a struggle for power. Not necessarily power for oneself; it can be a struggle in support of someone else. If the meaning and the aim of political activity is not for power, then it's not politics. It's fake. Or else the person making such a statement is simply not being honest with themselves and those around them.

People fight for power for two reasons. For some, having power is an end in itself. For others, power is a tool for achieving other aims. Putting it simply, you can divide politicians into pragmatists, who need nothing more than power itself, and ideologues, for whom achieving power is simply the start of a process. These divisions are, of course, relative and not absolute, but it is useful to bear them in mind.

I was never interested in the concept of power as an end in itself; or as an attribute of the alpha-male; or as the possibility to dominate and enjoy an inflated position in the social hierarchy. I've been at the very top of society – and at the very bottom, too. I have long understood that formal power, there for all to see, is sometimes worth very little. And that real power, which is often hidden from public view, bears no relation to a public position in politics. For reasons that will be obvious, I was never interested in using politics as a way to get rich, either. I was, and remain, sufficiently wealthy not to have to think about where my daily bread was coming from, and in any case no one can ever earn all the money in the world.

But this wasn't the main point. I've always been very wary – and remain so – of people for whom politics is an end in itself. The problem is that such people have no convictions – nor can they have. Convictions would have made them vulnerable, and made it difficult for them to achieve their goals. In general, other things being equal, it's easier for an unprincipled person to come to power, as they are unencumbered by any considerations. Such a person can be 'in favour of Soviet power' at one moment and, at the next, against; and in either situation they usually win. When there are too many politicians like this, society tumbles into a long period of crises.

Politicians who have convictions are a different matter, although here, too, nothing is simple. If fanatics come to power holding ideas loaded with hatred for certain groups of people, then they become a threat not only to their own society but to mankind as a whole. Nevertheless, the world would remain stubbornly patriarchal if we didn't have people in power who hold convictions that express the desire to change society. So the issue as to whether or not I should be involved in politics always brought me back to the question as to whether or not I held worthy convictions for which it made sense for me to go into politics – in other words, to fight for power. Not necessarily for my own personal benefit, but for the benefit of those forces that my convictions supported.

When I was released from prison, I didn't see any particular reason as to why I should become involved in politics in Russia. I held the same general democratic opinions that were supported by hundreds of thousands of other Russians with liberal-minded views. Naturally, I agreed with virtually nothing in the political course that Putin was pursuing, but I wasn't unique in that. I could express my convictions simply by supporting those whose opinions were close to mine, and this is what I did, even when I was in jail. There was absolutely no need for me to get involved in politics to do this. I didn't think that I could add anything substantially new or different from what others were already saying and doing. However, the situation changed shortly after my release.

Literally two months after I was forced to leave Russia against my will, the country became a very different place. Or, to be more precise, it went back to being what it had been before Mikhail Gorbachev introduced perestroika. It was as if the coup plotters of August 1991 had been resurrected and had finally decided to create an alternative version of history. The unsuccessful attempts to crush the revolution in Ukraine, which were followed by Russia's seizure of Crimea, which in turn was accompanied by the igniting of a war in the Donbas: all these events turned everything in Russia on its head. In the space of just a few months, politically Russia was thrown back decades. The first – and most important – reset had taken place. Putin and his circle wiped away everything that my generation had achieved when we had supported Gorbachev's and Yeltsin's attempts to change Russia. This went way beyond my personal conflict with Putin. Now we were talking about a fundamental difference in our views on the fate of Russia – its past, its present and its future. It was this that motivated me to become involved in politics, in a way that I hadn't intended to, neither when I was in prison nor at the time of my release. It came down to a very simple idea: I had to defend the beliefs and ideals of my generation of revolutionaries. To make it impossible for Russia ever again to give up its future by turning back to its past and falling into the same rut from which, through enormous efforts, we had managed to drag it out at the end of the 1980s.

But how can we do this? For the majority of those who share my views, the answer to this question sounded (and continues to sound) very straightforward: remove Putin and his clique from power. It sounds tempting, of course; but in reality it's not that simple. We got rid of Stalin – but Stalinism has returned. We disposed of Brezhnev – but stagnation has returned. We even overthrew the autocracy – and one hundred years later we're living under an autocratic system.

I have absolutely no doubts that we can get rid of Putin. In any case, sooner or later he'll depart this life: there are no immortal dictators. But Putinism, Stalinism and autocracy will keep returning to Russia again and again just as long as the sociopolitical and institutional preconditions exist for them. Although it's always easier and more convenient to personalize evil, it's not really about the individuals, but about the objective preconditions that allow anyone who reaches the pinnacle of power in Russia to become a Putin, a Brezhnev or a Stalin. This works as predictably as the laws of physics. Whether it's a revolutionary or an innovator or a liberator who comes to power, they all end up as a dictator, a satrap and someone who throttles freedom while desperately hanging on to power together with a pathetic cabal of corrupt henchmen. It is irrelevant who this individual is, because the reality of life in Russia breaks anyone. A specific example is that it wasn't a case of Putin breaking Russia, but of traditional Russia crushing Putin under its own weight. It was this understanding that Russia always seems doomed to repeat its own history that led me to seek a proper solution to this threat.

Gradually I've come to the deep conviction that the existing form of power in Russia simply maintains the traditional system of autocracy, and that, without revolutionary change, it will be impossible to escape from this autocratic trap. I've come to the conclusion that, given Russia's historical traditions and experience of politics, only a parliamentary form of government would be acceptable. Of course, we're talking here about a proper parliamentary republic, and not the rubber-stamp version that was typical of the Soviet 'parliament'.

In Russia, any other form of government, whereby all the executive functions of power are in the hands of the formal head of state, would inevitably sooner or later lead to the re-emergence of an autocratic and totalitarian regime. This would be for the simple reason that the cultural, economic and sociopolitical restrictions that prevent a state from sliding into the bog of authoritarianism are simply too underdeveloped in Russia. Any individual, even the weakest, who found themselves at the top of the pyramid of power, would not be able to stop themselves from being seduced into crushing that pyramid beneath them. This makes it essential to slice the top off this pyramid.

I see my mission as follows: to convince those who share my ideals and wish to see Russia free – not just for a couple of months or even years, but for decades to come – that this can be achieved, but only if we build a genuine federal parliamentary republic in Russia, with a developed system of local

self-governance at the municipal level. It is vital to rid ourselves
of a dictator; it is vital to investigate the crimes committed by
this regime; it is vital to re-establish even the most basic democratic norms in the country and to bring back justice and the
rule of law. And what is even more vital is that this be carried
out in such a way that everything that we put back cannot be
instantly lost once more. That is possible only by moving to a
parliamentary republic.

Building such a republic in Russia is far more complicated
than overturning Putin's regime. It calls for a genuine revolution, one that doesn't simply scratch the surface of political
life, but that overturns the very foundations of the traditional
Russian way of life. A revolution such as this demands massive
efforts and sacrifices; it means taking risks and changing literally everything, from the bottom to the very top. But only such
an all-encompassing revolution can provide Russia with the
long-term immunity that it needs to rid itself of autocracy and
give it the opportunity to build a new way of life suitable for the
modern, postindustrial, global world.

It's important at this point to explain what I understand
by 'revolution'. I am absolutely convinced that revolution
in Russia is inevitable, and that it's desperately needed. This
doesn't alter my extreme dislike of revolutions in principle,
or my deep regret that Russia has gone so far down a historic dead-end that the only possible way out is through a
revolution. Any revolution represents a trial for a society, even
when it brings with it a wonderful future. At the same time,
a revolution does not necessarily mean street battles, storm-
ing buildings, seizing post-offices, bridges and the telegraph
office. Such events are not indicative of a revolution, but of an
uprising. Yes, such incidents often accompany a revolution,
but they are not essential and, what's more, are not the main
component of a revolution.

What I understand by 'revolution' is a total reset of the fundamental principles of the life of a society, which completely

alters the course of that society's historical development. Whether such a reset of the fundamentals is accompanied by social explosions or whether it passes off without so much as a whimper are secondary questions. Most important of all is the result. In my opinion, Russia's move to become a parliamentary republic is only the tip of the iceberg. By 'parliamentary republic', I mean the country being run by a government made up of representatives of a coalition of parties that controls a parliament constituted by free and fair elections, and which, in turn, represents a genuinely wide majority of society. At the foundation of such a republic lie fundamental changes to the most varied aspects of the life of society, the implementation of which is essential in order that the system of parliamentary democracy remain sustainable and stable. The most important of all these changes is the switch to a genuinely federal system and the self-governance of cities. Only the cities can provide the political basis for a stable parliamentary republic.

In the case of Russia, a parliamentary republic and federalism are inseparable from one another. In order to drag Russia out of the rut of autocracy and place it firmly on a stable democratic trajectory, there has to be a move to a parliamentary republic. And in order to ensure that this parliamentary republic does not become yet another façade for autocracy, it must be reinforced by a federal system.

This is already a profound revolution: a country that for centuries has been accustomed to see itself from the top down must learn to look at itself from the bottom up. The logic here is simple. There are practically no democratic political traditions in Russia; what there have been are basically anti-democratic. Civil society didn't succeed in establishing itself properly, and today it's been practically wiped out. Even if favourable – close to ideal – conditions were to arise (and I seriously doubt that this is possible), the re-establishment of civil society even to the levels previously achieved would take years. And this is bearing in mind that the previous level of civil society was very basic. At the federal level, just as at the local level, there is no party system. All the existing parties are either fake – created or dominated by the authorities themselves – or they're marginal groups, united around their petty leaders and holding no serious weight among the majority of the population.

In such conditions, from where can a parliamentary system come with the stability needed to be an alternative to autocracy? Where can we find strength in a world of weakness? Only in the regions. It is only the regional elites, with their local interests, their local self-awareness and their regional links that have been built up over centuries, that have the ability in modern Russia to be the potential subjects – rather than the objects – of politics. If these elites were to support a parliamentary republic, it would come about. If they don't, it will simply disappear like yet another mirage of Russian history. A parliamentary republic is possible only if there is a proper federal structure, when local finances – and local life in general – are governed by those who live in the locality.

Why is the issue of federalism so important for Russia? It's because, with its cultural, religious and, of course, economic pluralism, Russia can be a unified state only under the cruellest of dictatorships, which crushes and levels out all local characteristics. Without such a dictatorship it's impossible to bring under a single umbrella places as disparate as Moscow and Grozny, Kazan and Magadan, Kaliningrad and Khabarovsk, St Petersburg and Kemerovo. If we wish to have even a hint of democracy in Russia, we must allow for the existence of pluralism – and not simply economic, but political, too. Incidentally, the Russian Empire that is so revered by Putin's followers was politically pluralistic. For centuries, the thoroughly European system of self-governance in Finland existed alongside the medieval khanates of Central Asia. Democracy in Russia means pluralism; and in modern times political pluralism can be achieved only through federalism.

Achieving this, however, is no easy task. Why is it that Russia has always been an overly-centralized state? Because if the centre showed any weakness and handed any significant autonomy over to the regions, petty little tsars would rise up in these regions, each of whom would prove to be greedier and more evil than the tsar in Moscow. So the people would then ask Moscow to help defend them from these regional satraps and the bandits whom they cultivated around them. And the power of the centre always relied on this. A weak tsar led to strong petty tsars, while a strong tsar meant the petty tsars were weak. How can this vicious circle be broken?

There is a way out. We need to introduce a third element, a force that is independent of these two extremes. This is something that everyone knows very well, because it's the very force that, in recent years, the Putin regime has been trying above all else to crush. It is local (municipal) self-governance. A regional governor who's taken power into his own hands while the centre was looking the other way can be stopped by an independent and autonomous mayor or head of a local administration. If local self-governance restricts the powers of the regional petty tsar, he or she will be obliged to become a regional constitutional monarch. And local self-governance will instinctively seek the support of Moscow, thus strengthening central government. This will help to even out the system, because it will bring in the checks and balances that are essential for creating a genuine democracy.

The space for an independent judiciary arises only when this triangle of local self-governance, regional governor and central government is developed. By definition, the relationship between the three cannot be ideal. There will either be constant war between them, or there will have to be an arbiter acceptable to all. It is absolutely impossible for there to be an independent legal system if the need for it is not recognized by those in a position of strength. Apart from the united local elites, there is no strong side in modern Russia: they've all been squeezed out. The centre, the regions and local self-governance will need rules together with an arbiter who can ensure that they are followed. In such a situation, perhaps the idea of a genuine independent judiciary might take root in Russia for the first time.

The arrival of a proper system of justice will mark the start of a gradual massive change in the relationship between the citizen and the state, and will create the conditions for the restoration (or, to be more accurate, building once more from scratch) of civil society in Russia. Progress in this will lead eventually to the final result: freedom, human rights, free and fair elections based on political competition, and stable institutions that support a state governed by the rule of law. But none of this, and much more besides, will come all at once. Such an outcome can be achieved only by following a chain of events step by step. And the most important link in this chain, I believe, is the path to a parliamentary republic.

It is specifically this path – and not 'a battle with a bloody regime' – that represents my goal, the pursuit of which has drawn me into politics. But the move towards it will not be swift and will require a great deal of patience.

Unfortunately, defining precisely the goal towards which we're heading doesn't guarantee that we'll end up exactly where we want to be. We have to be aware of what lies ahead of us on this path. Clearly, we cannot expect anything good as we begin our move away from the point to where Putin and his friends have brought us. Many of the prerequisites that are essential for the establishment of democracy in Russia simply don't exist. This is often ignored by many very honourable people, who are idealists in the best sense of the word, and who really want things to be better – but in the depths of their souls they realize that things will simply stay the same as they always have been. On the one hand, we have a terror machine served by an enormous number of functionaries who won't give up their positions even after Putin goes. And, on the other, we have a frightened society that has been oppressed by this terror and has lost its stable social connections, and a quantitatively reduced and qualitatively degraded elite. Obviously, we're not going to be able to jump across this ravine in one leap. We cannot avoid a period of transition during which the remnants of Putin's old society will be quashed, while zones for the growth of a new society are created. This idea is there for all to see, yet as a rule it's ignored in the general discussion about Russia's future. But from the practical point of view, it is the structure of society in this period of transition that's the most pressing issue today.

The point is that any kind of transition in Russia, no matter where it comes from or where it's going to, is like being in an enchanted forest, in which it's easier to lose oneself forever than it is to escape from it. What's more, no one has yet managed to escape from it in exactly the way they'd planned. This is why the period of transition has to be considered very seriously. We can be sure of only one thing: the time available for the post-Putin transition will be very limited. It must not last for more than two years, because any longer will mean that whatever political force takes Putin's place will not be able to maintain the people's trust. If the transitional, or interim, government doesn't manage to change anything in two years, then one of two things will inevitably happen. Either it will have to introduce a cruel dictatorship for an unspecified length of time, or it will be swept away by the people. This is because during the period of transition it will be essential for the government to introduce a whole host of unpopular measures in the most difficult of circumstances. And this is even before we take into account such complicating factors as the resistance of the old ruling clans and the likely fall in the standard of living that accompanies virtually every revolution. A compromise must be reached with society.

Thus, it is essential to construct a sturdy institutional framework for democracy in Russia. In my view this means creating a parliamentary republic, as well as a return to federalism and self-governance under the rule of law. Paradoxically, the question as to whether or not these long-term political goals are achievable depends on the ability of the interim government to obtain the trust of the majority in the short term. Without this, they won't be able to carry through effective – albeit in some aspects unpopular – policies, aimed at quelling the resistance of the old clans and establishing the basis for a new statehood.

If the interim government succeeds in establishing a strict new course then it would be realistic to believe that the long-term goals could be achieved. If, however, it's unable to do this, and it slips into populism by simply carrying out the immediate wishes of the people, then we can forget about such ambitions. People's trust must be lasting, drawn out over a long period. It's not difficult to gain the support of the majority over a short period of time. People grow weary of dictatorial regimes and in certain circumstances it takes just a spark to ignite passive dislike into active hatred. But such flare-ups quickly die down and the people can swiftly discard their new leaders. This is the weakness of Maidan-style uprisings: the explosion happens easily enough, but the strength of the explosion is insufficient to carry matters through to their conclusion. In order to obtain lasting support, different, systemic decisions are needed that do not simply take advantage of the anger that's been building up over a long period like social dynamite.

Considering all this, today we can at last make an accurate diagnosis of the 1990s. Surprisingly, that period has now once again become a subject of heated discussion. At that time, attempts to carry out coherent reforms failed. In my opinion, this was specifically because the reformers ignored the essential task of enlisting society's solid support. They naively believed that they could carry out changes while ignoring the views of the majority. At best, they assumed that they would remain neutral; in the worst case, they thought they could ride roughshod over any opposition. They chose a course of action

that appealed ideologically to a small section of society that
shared their radical Westernized views. The economic beneficiaries of the reforms were also a very mixed – and at the same
time tiny – group. Not only did the majority of the population
suffer significant economic hardship from these changes, but
the values that the reformers were preaching remained foreign
to them. The inevitable outcome of such a situation was that
society was alienated from the government and from the path
it was following. The consequences of this alienation were
reflected in the mass support for Putin's essentially counterrevolutionary, reactionary political course. If we don't want
to repeat this scenario in the future, we must not repeat the
errors of the 'nineties.

An exceedingly difficult task will present itself from the
outset to the interim government: in a situation where there is
a deep economic crisis and a fragmented society that is teeter-
ing on the edge of civil confrontation, how can problems be
solved that have built up over many decades? How can such a
government win the support of society for its actions?

If we put to one side any ideas of a quick fix based on a general
dislike of the old regime (and experience shows that such dislike doesn't last long), then all that remains is to put into action
a 'left-wing plan' that would at least satisfy the fundamental
economic needs of the majority of the population. It's essential that the majority believe that the government's actions
strategically match their own long-term economic interests.
Only then will they be prepared to back the government in
its difficult journey through the period of transition. In other
words (and many people still fail to accept this), there's a fairly
simple constraint to any deep change in Russia: it will have to
be carried out along with a 'left-wing plan'. By 'left-wing plan',
I mean that it must be geared towards broad-scale social and
economic needs; as opposed to a 'right-wing plan' that satisfies
the needs of a minority. Had the reformers in the 1990s not
ignored the social needs of the majority of the people, it is

quite possible that today we would not be trying to solve the problem of Putinism. If those who have set themselves the task of carrying out a political battle with the regime once again ignore the social and economic needs of the majority, they will never achieve their political goals.

Nowadays, everyone understands this. Today, there is no opposition force that wouldn't promise the Russian people social benefits and economic well-being along with political freedom and a state governed by the rule of law. Nevertheless, people don't rush to believe such promises. For some, it's because the 1990s are still fresh in their minds; for others, it's because there are few concrete details in such promises, and much of what is said is unrealistic given the current state of the economy.

In order to win enough trust from the majority to carry out far-reaching changes, people shouldn't be given promises of a wonderful life in some far-off future; rather, there should be guarantees that will work right now. Strange as it may seem, such guarantees do exist, and can be presented to the people by an interim government in exchange for long-term support of a reformist path. This involves returning to the people what was taken from them in the 1990s: namely, the benefit from the extraction of natural resources, known as resource rent, and a fair distribution of property.

Resource rent is the principal source of wealth in Russia, both private and public. Officially, resource rent today is controlled by the state; but, in reality, it's controlled by the mafia cabal that's replaced the state. All ideas that are put forward regarding the fate of resource rent come back to one point: whatever force replaces the Putin regime has to ensure that the distribution of resource rent is done more fairly than it is today. In other words, that the people receive more than they do now. But since the Russian population has grown used to regarding anything related to the state with deep mistrust, they don't believe in this crock of gold at the end of the rainbow, either.

But a completely different approach can be taken, one that completely excludes the state from its role as the distributor of resource rent among the population. In recent years, everyone has realized that there are two insoluble problems in Russia: pensions and the unfair distribution of profits from the sale of natural resources. So why not solve one problem with the help of the other? Why not send the proceeds from energy sales (which, in any case, are accounted separately from the rest of the income items of the budget) to citizens' individual savings accounts, which could be held directly in the Treasury? The sum that's needed to pay fair pensions is almost exactly the same as the amount that goes into the budget from resource rent. So linking together is totally logical. In one fell swoop, the Russian people would be able directly to control resource rent, and would stop feeding a gigantic bureaucracy and the mafia that's attached itself to it. This is something that both can and should be done immediately after the interim government takes over. It would open up a channel of political opportunity for implementing difficult changes. This is the most important thing; but there is something else as well.

Clearly, it will be impossible in practice to restore trust between the state and society in the near future, unless the consequences of the one-sided privatizations of the 1990s are removed. The trauma that followed the birth of privatization will prevent the introduction of any measures to improve the health of the economy. It means that there's no trust in society, not only for the government, but for the very idea of private property. Yet private property lies at the heart of any constitutionally governed state. Largely thanks to the experience of privatization in the 'nineties, the majority of the population see all private property in Russia as the result of an unfair distribution of state assets. What's more, this is also partly a reflection of today's situation, since a significant portion of public wealth is controlled by a small criminal segment that has crushed the state.

There are two reasons why no progress can be made along the path to democratic reform unless this totally parasitic ownership of property is wiped out. First, if this property remains in the hands of the collective beneficiaries of the Putin regime, it will be used to block any constructive activity attempted by the interim government. And, second, unless this property is confiscated, it will be impossible to earn society's trust; society won't support any government that leaves this money in the hands of these people.

Therefore, the second essential social measure of the interim government must be the expropriation of this parasitic capital from the Putin clan. The assets that are seized from them must be placed into management by public investment funds under the control of parliament. The income from the activity of these funds should be directed towards additional funding for social projects. First and foremost, this should be for education and health care. This money can be placed in individual savings accounts that will be opened for every citizen. This could be considered as a compensatory measure, to right the wrongs that were committed by the state under its privatization programme. So it would be a step towards re-establishing socioeconomic justice.

In effect, Russia today lives under a state of emergency. There exists a regime of political terror. Any practical resistance to the authorities is paralysed. However, experience shows that this cannot continue forever. Any closed system ultimately contains within itself the reason for its collapse. Putin's regime will be no exception. And even if right now it's difficult to shape the longevity of this regime, it's entirely possible to influence the pace of the post-regime recovery. This will largely depend on the intensity of the reaction by the elites to what is happening; on how much preparation is done to rethink Russian history; on there being a clear and achievable goal from those seeking change; and, even more importantly, on there being a detailed road-map for change.

The normalization process after the fall of the regime will be made much simpler and swifter if a provisional consensus can be reached by society on all these points. The lack of such a consensus, and especially the lack of an actual plan around which consensus can be reached, will have a seriously adverse effect on society's chances of repairing itself. Indeed, it may even make this impossible. Circumstances today are such that, for a period of time – and this could be quite a long time – spiritual and intellectual opposition may prove to be virtually the only form of resistance possible for the majority of those citizens who are opposed to the regime. But the 'otherworldliness' and seeming abstractness of such resistance don't lessen its historic significance. On the contrary, this is exactly where the frontline of the battle for the future of Russia lies today. Every action begins with a word; and it's vital that this word be the right one and that it hit the target.

In today's Russia there's no place for politics and no motives for engaging in politics. But there will be in the future Russia. And it's the thought of a Russia that confines Putinism to the past that inspires me to take up political activity. That future looks complicated. Putin will leave Russia with a difficult legacy that will make future progress hard. The path will be sown with the kind of historical traps that Russia has already fallen into on a number of occasions, and it's ended up being stuck in them for decades.

I am convinced that the re-formation of Russia into a parliamentary and genuinely federal republic with strong local self-governance is the fulcrum that can provide the starting point from where we can cast off the curse of autocracy forever. At the same time, I'm aware that reaching this starting point can be done in Russia only by 'driving in the left lane'. My political goal today is to create a wide consensus in society both for the goal itself and for the methods by which it will be reached.

Part I

How Do We Get Rid of the Old Dragon?

The vast majority of people live comfortably alongside the dragon until it comes to the crunch, that being the day when they or their loved ones are killed, arrested or kicked out onto the street from their cosy little comfort zone. Love for the dragon is the natural state of affairs for the average person, which immediately becomes the main problem in any transitional period from dictatorship to democracy. It's easier to get rid of the dragon than it is to defeat the ordinary person's devotion to it. For this reason, getting rid of the dragon is not simply a lovely, one-act revolutionary show that ends with happy and joyous fireworks. It's a drama that takes place over many acts, and has a complicated and sometimes tragic theme. And in each act of this drama, its actors must overcome difficult dilemmas, many of which don't have straightforward solutions.

1

The Strategy for Victory: Peaceful Protest or Peaceful Uprising?

What should be the strategy for victory in the battle against despotism? People who lived in the eighteenth, nineteenth or, especially, the twentieth century would find it easy to answer this question. The strategy for victory is revolution.

But what sort of revolution? A violent one, of course. Marx wrote that revolution is the midwife of history. And the nineteenth-century US president, Abraham Lincoln, expressed it thus: 'Whenever they shall grow weary of the existing government, they can exercise their constitutional right of amending it, or their revolutionary right to dismember or overthrow it.'

The right of the American people to rise up against those who have usurped power is enshrined in the United States' Declaration of Independence. Lenin and his supporters regarded revolution as the fundamental source of law and called for the enemies of the revolution to be judged according to their revolutionary legal consciousness. It was clear who the enemy was and what needed to be done with them.

But in the final quarter of the twentieth century, everything became much more complicated. Revolutions, which over the course of 200 years had caused rivers of blood to flow across

Europe, became unfashionable. And the collapse of the USSR and of the regimes in Eastern Europe that were linked to the Soviet Union created the illusion that victory over tyrants could be achieved without the use of violence. Perhaps not immediately, but, ultimately, violence was removed from the strategy of the struggle against despotism as something that was undesirable and even unacceptable. So what then was left in this strategy?

Peaceful protest was seen as the only acceptable and universal strategy for all times and in all situations. The aim was not simply a revolution, but it had to be a velvet revolution, a revolution in kid gloves. From now on, protest could not involve violence, even if this violence were to be directed against a tyrant and his henchmen who had drowned the country in blood.

Up to a certain point, this strategy of non-resistance to evil by violence worked; at least, that was how it seemed from the sidelines. The velvet revolutions developed into colour revolutions (although it would be more accurate to describe them as 'flower revolutions': 'the Rose Revolution', 'the Carnation Revolution', and so on). Colour revolutions became the successful political technology, which led to the careful removal from power of authoritarian regimes without serious bloodshed – at least at the moment when power passed into the hands of the opposition. In the twenty years that passed from the time of the 'self-dissolution' of the USSR and the tearing down of the Berlin Wall, the standard set by the colour revolutions became, first of all, the model for revolution, and then revolutionary dogma. But the very formation of a dogma leads inevitably to stagnation.

It's necessary here to point out one thing: no revolution, even a velvet one, takes place without violence, or, more often, without a clear and imminent threat of violence, which leads the regime to prefer to seek a compromise. It's this preparedness of the regime to compromise, and not the desire on the part of the revolutionaries to find a compromise with the regime at any cost, that makes velvet revolutions possible. As a result, such revolutions succeed only when they are up against outdated dictatorships – authoritarian regimes that are run by the children or even the grandchildren of their founders.

Recently, there was a revolutionary situation in Belarus. At first, the opposition tried to solve the situation by employing traditional rules, using the methods of colour revolutions: coordination, mobilization, solidarity, psychological pressure and the moral support of the West, occasionally strengthened by a little financial help.

In the past, as a rule, this set of actions had proved sufficient for a dictatorship to capitulate. But in Belarus, things didn't quite work out that way. The opposition was coordinated: it mobilized, it demonstrated unprecedented solidarity, it brought powerful psychological pressure to bear, and it had the support of the West; but all this came to nought. The regime drowned the opposition in violence, and the support of the West was more than made up for on the other side by the help received from Russia. The constant attempts to bring people out onto the streets have done nothing to bring the opposition any closer to success, as a result of which general dissatisfaction with the outcome of the revolution only continues to grow.

Against this background, both in Belarus itself and beyond, there was inevitably a discussion about the strategy of protest in a situation where regimes fail to give ground, and where there's no possibility of outside intervention (clearly, no one was going to start a nuclear war with Russia for the sake of the Belarusians' freedom).

This gave rise, on the one hand, to doubts as to whether adopting solely peaceful methods for the struggle really is a universal and effective solution in any revolutionary situation. On the other hand, there were concerns that calling for non-peaceful methods could lead to the protest being discredited in the eyes of both the population and the international community. This would lead, in its turn, to inevitable defeat. So it was that peaceful and non-peaceful methods of protest came to be seen in juxtaposition to one another. In my view, this is a completely false dilemma.

In principle, can there be nonviolent protest in a non-democratic state? Under despotism there are no permitted legal boundaries for protest; that's why it's despotism. Any citizen genuinely protesting against a dictatorial regime (and not simply taking part in a mock protest as agreed with the authorities) is already breaking the law. If rallies, marches, demonstrations, pickets and other forms of public political activity are forbidden, then a single step out onto the streets, even with the most peaceful of intentions, can be dangerous, because it's likely to lead to provocation of violence by the authorities and, in turn, to resistance, even if it's passive, such as someone being beaten by the police protecting their head from the blows of the truncheons.

So under a dictatorship, the types of protest that we automatically call peaceful or non-peaceful don't differ from each other at all. Any kind of public protest against the usurpation of power has the potential to be non-peaceful, even though the level of violence can differ from case to case, from virtually nothing to something serious.

In some circumstances, the level of violence that is acceptable for the participants may be very low; in others, it could be quite high. But in all cases, the threshold is not zero. If it were, people just simply wouldn't take part in protest actions. When we have dictatorship on one side and genuine protest against it on the other, we're allowing for at least the possibility of a violent clash by calling on people to disobey the laws laid down by the dictatorship.

I believe that the question about peaceful or non-peaceful protest overshadows a much more significant question, and leads the discussion off on a tangent. The question is whether in principle we consider that revolutionary violence is legitimate. It's only when we've answered this question that we can proceed to the next one: what is the desirable or non-desirable form that said violence can take? In my opinion, there can be only one answer: yes, revolutionary violence is legitimate.

If we properly analyse the position of those in favour of only peaceful protest then it quickly emerges that, more often than not, behind the beautiful and peace-loving words lies an attempt to defend the idea of the illegitimacy of revolutionary violence in principle. This is a dangerous delusion. If you regard peaceful protest as meaning that you reject on principle any revolutionary violence (and that is how many people naively see it), then you will be in good company with any dictator. But doing battle with the dictatorship will be completely impossible.

Throughout the history of mankind, no dictatorship has disappeared without coming under the clear or hidden threat of force. No dictator ever stepped down just because they were tired. If it wasn't violence itself, then it was at least the threat of violence that always played a decisive role in the victory of the revolution. It's another matter that the threat of violence has nearly always been more effective than blatant violence.

This is not simply a question of humanity. If a revolution starts with violence, it will end with it, too. And if a revolution ends in violence, then that will never actually be the end of it. A violent revolution almost inevitably produces a dictatorship in its wake that sets out to crush any counterrevolution. This must be borne in mind by anyone who – contrary to those who believe only in peaceful protest – calls for a swift transition to a violent struggle.

Nevertheless, as the experience of Belarus showed (and bearing in mind that the Russian experience promises to be even more striking), if the regime is prepared to open fire on its own people, then a demonstrative and early refusal by the opposition to use violence as a way of seizing power will be counterproductive. Unless it is supported by the threat of

direct foreign intervention, restricting protest to simply apply-
ing psychological pressure can never bring down a regime that
is prepared to go to any lengths to stay in power. This is the
case even if the protest has the broad support of the majority of society. For this reason, the concept of peaceful protest
as a total and absolute rejection of revolutionary violence is
nothing more than dogma. If you turn away completely from
violence, then you turn away from revolution.

In reality, not only is revolutionary violence legitimate, but
historically it has always and everywhere proved to be a source
of the new legitimacy. Revolution and constitution always go
hand in hand. Had there been no violent revolutions in the
world, constitutional order would never have been established
anywhere. This must be borne in mind even when you look
back over many centuries.

If the constitutional order collapses, then frequently the
only realistic way to restore it has been to return to the use
of revolutionary violence. This was why the old constitutions
contained the people's revolutionary right to rise up, and
devoted so much attention to the people's right to bear arms.
Anyone who tried to seize power had to understand that anything taken *from* the people by force could be taken *back* by
the people by force, because a nation that rose up had greater
legitimacy than a despotic regime had. These are hard truths.
But they are the ABCs of revolution – and they need to be
learnt by heart. If, that is, you wish to be victorious.

However, recognizing the legitimacy of revolutionary violence as a means of struggle against a dictatorship does not
mean that you're immediately ready in practice to resort to
this violence. Recognizing the possibility and the legitimacy of
using violence in a revolutionary struggle with a dictatorship is
a strategic question. Employing or not employing violence in a
concrete situation and, if you do choose to employ it, to what
extent and in what ways – that's a question of revolutionary
tactics, and that can be decided in very different ways.

Often, the deliberate refusal to escalate the violence in order to avoid massive casualties is the only correct solution, especially when the majority isn't ready to take action if there's no revolutionary situation in the country. But transforming this decision into a dogma, a conviction that, in any circumstances, your protest must remain peaceful, is the same as voluntarily laying down your arms before the dictator and, in effect, giving up any realistic struggle for power. The regime should always be under pressure, aware that if any force is used there will be a counterforce, and that every crime will be punished. Only in such circumstances will those in opposition to the regime have any hope of success.

Nevertheless, peaceful pressure is not always as peaceful as its proponents might wish it to be. A peaceful protest that doesn't involve any violence can still burn up the resources of those in power and limit their opportunities to use violence themselves. This can happen for a wide variety of reasons. It may be because of the collapse of policing structures, or because of the depletion of material resources (in such a situation, a strike can be a very real use of force), or for a variety of other reasons. However, there is the danger that, if a regime collapses because it's run out of material resources, then the ones who gain most on the battlefield will be the looters, be they criminals or invaders. In this case, the protest movement will find itself having to use violence against a third party.

One thing alone is clear. The protest cannot be held back from within through self-censorship. If the revolution has a built-in restriction on how fast it can go, it will never get off the ground. Once they've started, the leaders of the protest must always be ready to take the next step. Once you've called people out onto the streets, then you have to accept that, by that action, you've already made revolutionary violence possible. It's a different matter if, as a tactical move, you call upon your supporters temporarily to hold back.

Calling for violence when there's no revolutionary situation is just as much a betrayal of protest as refusing to use violence in a revolutionary situation, when this is essential to bring the revolution to an end. The latter would be the same as leaving the movement leaderless and at the mercy of fate. As a rule, that will lead to the swift defeat of the revolution and even greater violence and casualties, only no longer on the part of the revolution but, rather, that of the counterrevolution. This is why protest should, of course, always try to remain peaceful; and it will remain so if there is convincing evidence that you are prepared to respond to violence with violence if necessary.

2

Bringing the Protesters Together: Many Parties or a Single Party?

Everyone knows the well-worn metaphor of the broken arrows. It's been passed down through the ages. A wise leader (or a tsar) first demonstratively shows how easy it is to break single arrows one by one. He then helplessly throws up his hands after trying to break a whole quiver of such arrows all at once. It's become a hackneyed image; but its basic message remains true. When any kind of protest is united, that unity is the key feature that makes it effective. Few would argue with this; but everyone tends to understand in their own way just what that unity actually means. There is the kind of unity with many different voices, and there is the kind of unity where everyone needs to sing with one voice.

This is exactly the question that the democratic opposition in Russia is facing today. When they speak, the leaders of all the even remotely significant protest movements say they are in favour of unity. Indeed, it would be very odd to hear them declaim that they're against a wide front in the struggle with the dictatorship. Yet many of those who talk about unity are guided in practice by a different principle, one that was put forward in similar historical circumstances by Lenin: 'Before we can unite . . . we must first of all draw firm and definite lines of demarcation.' The danger of this slogan is that, in the process of putting all their efforts into demarcation, the ultimate goal of unity slips into the background. This is exactly what we see happening today in Russia.

If we look back at history, we can see that protest movements have succeeded by following various paths. Among these, we can pick out two types of successful revolutions. Some were carried out by close-knit groups of likeminded people, not only united by their similar political views, but also organized along pseudo-military lines. This gave them a structure on which to build the new state after their victory. Other successful revolutions were carried out by a wide coalition of the most varied political forces, linked by only a fragile organizational bond. This bond rarely survived the actual revolution.

If we look more closely at this, we realize that very often the tactical tasks of the revolution, such as the seizure and consolidation of power, were carried out more effectively by pseudo-military, conspiratorial organizations more akin to religious sects in their structure than by political parties in the strict sense of that term. But the strategic tasks that the revolutions had before them, notably tasks of a democratic nature, were better solved where a coalition of diverse forces stood at their head, having been brought together by the moment and the circumstances.

Knowing this, you might think that all responsible political forces would try to create a broad coalition. But in practice this doesn't happen. Either coalitions aren't formed or, if they are, they quickly fall apart. Unfortunately, there are strong objective reasons for this. History shows that the more aggressive the dictatorship and the more ruthless the regime, the fewer chances there are for a coalition to come together and triumph. This is understandable. The regime recognizes that the unity of the opposition forces represents the greatest threat to its existence, and so does everything in its power to prevent the opposition from uniting, including supporting secessionist sentiments within the opposition itself. If the regime has to choose between *irreconcilable elements* and *the most irreconcilable elements* among the opposition, strangely enough they tend to choose the latter, even though this risks bringing about their own downfall, as has already happened once in Russian history, at the start of the twentieth century.

We must never forget that there is not only a tradition of autocracy in Russia, there is also a tradition of Bolshevism – that is, of sectarianism and schism within the revolutionary movement. Each of these traditions is closely linked to the other. In the country's history, Bolshevism has played no less a tragic role than autocracy, which it first destroyed, then re-incarnated in a more sophisticated form. For the vast majority of our contemporaries, Bolshevism and Communism are one and the same thing. But this is not the case. It's possible not to be a Communist – even to be an anti-Communist – and at the same time remain a Bolshevik. What's more, if Communism in Russia appeared largely by chance, Bolshevism grew out of the very roots of Russian culture.

Bolshevism is a movement that developed out of Russian populism [through movements such as the *Narodniki* – Tr.], and not just out of liberal ideals. For Bolshevism, as for autocracy, it was the state that was the 'social demiurge', not society. But if autocracy aimed to preserve society unchanged with the help of the state, Bolshevism wanted to use the state to turn society inside out. The Bolsheviks never needed allies in power; they simply needed power itself. Bolshevism is very tenacious, and can take on the most unexpected forms; it encompasses not only Leninism and Stalinism, but also, for example, Yeltsinism in its most extreme form. Unfortunately, many of the reforms of the 1990s were carried out in the same cavalier Bolshevik ways as Soviet reforms had been, although at the time this was not so obvious. And today we can see the rise of neo-Bolshevik sentiments in the Russian protest movement. This philosophy and ideology are becoming increasingly attractive as the regime becomes ever more restrictive.

Neo-Bolshevism's strength lies in its being aimed at literally creating an army of likeminded people who are ready to act harmoniously and in an organized way as the unitary centre commands. Lenin called this 'a new type of party'. Such an army is much more effective than an amorphous and shaky coalition put together to solve political issues in a civil war being waged by a regime against its own people. But there's another side to the coin. War creates fertile ground for neo-Bolshevism to bloom in the lush colours of violence. That's the ideal environment for neo-Bolshevism, which is why – consciously or unconsciously – it's always geared up for war. Neo-Bolshevism's response to a civil war that a dictatorship has declared on the people is to launch its own civil war. It puts out a fire with return fire of its own.

The Bolshevik tradition in the Russian protest movement presupposes that the unity of the protest should depend on a single party. This means that the nucleus of the protest movement must be ideologically and organizationally homogeneous, governed from a single point at the centre by a leader or a group of leaders. The nucleus may have 'fellow travellers' on its periphery, but any alliance with them is merely temporary and opportunistic. For neo-Bolshevism, betrayal of such allies is the political and ethical norm. A reliable ally should totally merge into the party, politically and in an organizational sense. The party is not there to represent the interests of society, after all; it's meant to be the 'transmission belt' between the leadership and the revolutionary class.

Naturally, if we're talking about an armed uprising or a war, then organizing the protest movement this way is ideal. But the problem in such circumstances is that, for the neo-Bolsheviks, the war becomes an end in itself. If the situation develops relatively peacefully, they'll have no chance whatsoever of coming to power. Indeed, they cannot simply come to power; they can only seize power when things have broken down to such an extent that all the institutions of the state have ground to a halt. That's why the two principal slogans of neo-Bolshevism always have been, and remain, 'the worse things are, the better'; and 'anyone who is not with us is against us'.

Paradoxically, as a radical tendency in the protest movement, neo-Bolshevism assists the temporary stabilization and strengthening of the regime. Thanks to the neo-Bolsheviks, the only possible change can come about through a violent coup, carried out at the moment of the regime's final ruin. This happens when there's a total collapse as a result of war, a huge ecological disaster or some other similar catastrophe. Because neo-Bolshevism sees itself as the main beneficiary in such a situation, it stops protesters from uniting and prevents any handover of power that might take place before such a collapse, or at least in a less violent way. It extends the life of the regime in the belief that it will eventually bury it. It is because of this support that it's valued by the regime.

In most instances, neo-Bolshevism represents a dead-end for the protest movement, since the conditions necessary for its triumph simply don't align. But on those rare occasions when war or some other comparable catastrophic event brings down the regime, and the neo-Bolshevik sects are presented with the opportunity of a successful coup, it invariably ends in a civil war and a new dictatorship, sometimes even more cruel than the one it's replaced. This comes from the very nature of neo-Bolshevism, which believes it to be essential that only a small section of the population should seize and hold power. Is this the revolution that awaits Russia? Is such a victory over the current regime worth dying for?

An alternative to neo-Bolshevism could be a protest coalition: a multiparty, multifaceted protest; a collection of various political groups. Of course, a coalition is not the best form of organization in a war. But the basic principle of a coalition is this: better to unite sooner than to allow the situation to become worse. Uniting the opposition creates the conditions for a change of regime before the moment of its natural collapse. The price of the fall of the regime is measured in the number of lives victory will cost. And we cannot be indifferent to what this final price will be.

A coalition is always a compromise. A coalition brings together radical forces, less radical forces and even those who may lean towards cooperating with the regime. Neo-Bolshevism is inevitably and exclusively radical. Yes, it also seeks compromises, but only tactical ones, designed to achieve a particular result, after which they'll deal with these fellow travellers. This is why all historical alliances that the Bolsheviks have formed have always ended badly for their temporary allies. The principal slogan of a coalition is in direct contrast to that of the neo-Bolsheviks: 'All who are not against us, are with us.' We don't want the result of the revolution to be post-revolutionary ruin, but a post-revolutionary democratic state, governed by the rule of law.

If someone is prepared to make compromises before the revolution, they'll be ready to make them after the revolution, too. But someone who refuses to make compromises ahead of the revolution will be even less likely to agree to them after it, and will become a revolutionary dictator. In time, a revolutionary dictator becomes simply a dictator, and a new revolution will be needed in order to get rid of them. This is the vicious circle that Russia has been living in for more than a hundred years. And if the most radical revolutionaries are not prepared to unite with those who are neither radical nor revolutionaries, then that simply means that they are continuing to prepare the ground for an eternal Putin.

Of course, there are different sorts of compromises, too. We need to strike a happy medium between the kind of single party structure that leads to neo-Bolshevism, and the kind of multiparty structure that results in a mere talking-shop where nothing is done. There will be times in the revolutionary process when we will need military leaders. But alongside them there must always be an institution that gives legitimacy to the leaders' revolutionary authority and that prevents them from rising above the revolution and society.

The creation of a revolutionary coalition is the most important task of the opposition, notwithstanding its unpopularity among the protesters. In reality, a coalition will bring revolution closer by creating a protesting majority and, most importantly, a coalition guarantees that the revolution will not end up in a new dictatorship. Compromises will be possible and essential in order to create a coalition. As well as having a radical centre, every successful revolution has to have very broad and less radical support around it. That is what links the revolution to the people. Without this, success is impossible to achieve.

3

How to Cultivate Protest: Go Underground or Emigrate?

Protest is a subtle and complicated issue.

On the one hand, it's impossible to create it or artificially encourage it. It arises all by itself and follows its own trajectory. Protest leaders have to follow this trajectory carefully and try not only to move with it, but also anticipate each next step, so as always to be in the right place at the right time.

On the other hand, in order to be in a position to do this, it's essential to be in a state of permanent readiness, by maintaining links with the people and being fuelled by their energy, while providing them with ideological fuel. And leaders may have to be in this state of readiness – while being unable to act – for a long time. Years. Maybe even decades. It's not easy to do, either psychologically or purely technically.

Naturally, the question arises: where should the leaders be while they wait for the protest to gain sufficient strength to launch into its political orbit? This is a difficult question to answer today; and tomorrow it will be even harder. We've witnessed how, in just a few years, the regime in Russia has gone from being shamefacedly authoritarian to being openly fascist; and then, not stopping there, it has blatantly embraced

Nazism. I should add that my use of these terms is entirely notional, because we're talking here about something purely Russian, something that's grown out of the country's history; therefore, it can be compared only superficially with what we know from Europe's experience of fascism and Nazism. This will have a multitude of consequences, but one of the most important from the practical point of view is that, in this new situation, the possibilities for legal political activity will be, at the very least, severely limited, or they may even disappear altogether.

It is vital to be aware of this now and adjust our thinking appropriately. Many of the legal and semi-legal institutionalized methods of protest that we are used to today will simply disappear. I can foresee a situation in which all the reasonably convenient media platforms where one could more or less freely criticize the authorities may be shut down in the near future. For the Russian secret services, the internet will become the same kind of battlefield that short-wave radio was during the Cold War. The regime is going to jam the 'Voices' [one of the principal foreign radio stations that broadcast into the USSR was Voice of America; others included the BBC, Radio Liberty and Deutsche Welle – Tr.], while the people (or, to be more precise, the greatly diminished active segment of the population) are going to try to come up with new ways of obtaining the truth. The opposition may end up experiencing the same fate as the dissident movement, forced by repression to the very fringes of society.

There's no single view among the opposition as to where and how to carry on the struggle under such conditions (many are even trying to avoid looking into this scary future). All talk tends to focus on two options: emigration or going underground. There are those who consider that the only way to oppose the regime is to leave the country. Others, though, suggest that the sole way of maintaining the link with the protest movement is to stay in Russia.

As is often the case, both groups are right in their own way. It's essential to fight this neo-totalitarian dictatorship with all available means, both underground and in emigration. So rather than argue about where the real opponents of the regime should sit, we have to think right now about how best to unite the forces of all those who are working for Russia's future, both inside and outside the country. The best place for a member of the opposition is where they can be of maximum help for the cause at any given moment.

We have to begin by looking at modern-day reality. In the era of global electronic control, the possibilities for illegal underground work are going to be greatly restricted, not only compared to what the situation was like in Tsarist Russia, but even compared to the Soviet Union (although at the time it seemed that such possibilities could not be more limited). In order to be hidden from the view of the secret services nowadays, members of the opposition have to demonstrate all the skills of secret service agents. This is extremely difficult to accomplish in real life. By its very nature, the underground is a path that only a very few exceptional individuals can follow. You have to have a natural inclination for this sort of life, and ice in your veins. From the outset you have to be prepared to spend a huge amount of your life in prison, or even to die for the sake of an idea. Talk of having a wide underground movement is quite simply utopian.

So what does this leave? First and foremost, a game of cat and mouse with the authorities in the legal sphere. Even in the harshest totalitarian systems, the regime has to leave a few gaps for pseudo-civic legal activity. The regime will, of course, try to control this completely from within, but externally it's supposed to appear as the activity of working civic institutions. A classic example of this in Soviet times were the pseudo-civic organizations known as arts unions (of writers, artists, cinematographers, journalists, and so on). Later, during the years of perestroika, some of them did play a leading role in pushing forward changes in society. In the broad game of chess that the opposition is going to have to start playing with this regime – a regime that has finally put a halt to the legacy of Gorbachev and Yeltsin – every such union, every such 'cell' that has been created and been allowed to continue to exist by the authorities for its own purposes should be regarded as a tiny piece of society that must be taken over. If the opposition doesn't do this, this piece will remain in the hands of the authorities.

The regime is also constantly looking at the alignment of forces. It could simply ban everything; but the more it bans, the harder it becomes to control the situation. It has to find a balance. So it leaves a few gaps where it considers that the plusses outweigh the minuses. It's those places that the opposition should concentrate on, dashing from one to another. Because even as some windows are being closed, others will be opening.

Working in conditions of limited legality will impose certain barriers. Clearly, we'll have to learn again the language of Aesop's Fables and choose our words very carefully. Anyone who suggests they are seeking power will be wiped out by the regime, but some possibilities will remain open for those who are not aiming for power. Therefore, it will be essential to limit one's ambitions.

One of the opposition's main tasks will be to entice back those who have been recruited by the state. Those who are extremely intolerant towards those they consider as 'loyalists' have to start thinking about this right now. Today, it is only from abroad that the radical opposition is able to speak out in its own voice. Yet the oppositionists lump together anyone who doesn't share a radical opinion, anyone who's adapted to the regime or who partially accepts it, and, especially, anyone who is a part of the regime, albeit not one of the worst. And these people are all harshly criticized as collaborators. But this opportunity to speak in one's own voice may disappear altogether very soon, meaning that the only voices that will be heard are those in the grey area. If the opposition wants to continue to be heard, it has to learn to speak with those in the grey area.

When it comes to influencing public opinion, no kind of underground work can take the place of what can be done legally. The long history of dealing with totalitarianism bears this out. Therefore, striking alliances with those who are undecided is one of the most important conditions for success, as these are the very people who can open the way to a legal approach, even in the most adverse conditions. What is meant by 'alliances'? First, attracting onto our side those whom the regime still allows to write and to speak. Second, starting to work inside those organizations that the regime has created to give the impression of the existence of a civil society, and forming within them groups of sympathizers. And third, in developing independent work in those borderline fields that the regime finds it difficult to wipe out immediately: human rights, social assistance, charity, educational work, economic initiatives, and so on.

What else can the underground do? Undoubtedly, prepare public acts of protest. Not so as to seize power, but to show the flag and other symbols that will keep the movement alive. Of course, this also includes maintaining in readiness communication and organizational links so that, if there is any change in the political situation, they can emerge swiftly from underground and become a normal political organization.

Finally, there is assistance for those who have been arrested and for their families. In this instance, we must bear in mind that, in present circumstances, financing any illegal work from external sources will, in effect, be impossible, fraught as it is with instant disclosure and sanctions. So all local activists and organizations that have managed to survive will have to be largely self-financing. But this in itself will reduce the number of such organizations.

Nevertheless, if the Russian state continues to develop as we've seen in recent years, sooner or later the opposition will have to acknowledge that the focal point of its political work will have to take place abroad. They have to look at this soberly and start to prepare for it psychologically. Recent experience, including what happened in Belarus, illustrates that the only place that the coordinating hub of opposition activity can be based is outside the country. Any attempt to create it internally will be smashed by the regime. It's only abroad that the work of the independent opposition media can be fully rolled out, although the distribution of its content within Russia will be a separate challenge. (But in order to distribute something good, you still have first to produce it.) It's abroad, too, that projects to train the people who will be running the future Russia will have to be located. And it is there that the necessary financial resources can be mobilized and that Western public opinion can be influenced.

Of course, emigration is always a compromise. But the problem is that those who are going to try to live on inside the country will soon have to make even more of a compromise. I believe that we're going to have to change our usual attitude to political emigration as forced flight and stop dividing the opposition into categories of 'those on the ground' and 'those abroad'. In this way, emigration can simply be considered as a second front in the struggle against the regime; and if the situation becomes too dreadful, it may even become the main front. There must be clear mutual cooperation between those who are fighting inside the country and those carrying on the struggle from abroad. It's only with such cooperation that the opposition's two fronts can survive and operate.

But those who are operating abroad will have extra problems. The regime will inevitably describe these political emigrants as spies and saboteurs who are in the pay of foreign secret services. And that's only part of it. The fact is that political emigrants will certainly not have an easy relationship with the governments and secret services of those countries where they try to establish their bases. History has shown that European governments are not exactly thrilled about having opponents of the Russian regime operating on their territories, because it's a headache they could do without. It also creates extra problems in their relations with the Kremlin.

It seems clear that there's going to have to be a division of labour. From a certain point, any open discussion about the model for the new Russia will be possible only somewhere where the dictatorship is not operating. But the spread of free ideas from outside will be difficult. It will be done by those who are courageous enough to carry on the struggle inside the country. We have to be prepared for a significant period of time during which the protest will have to be kept in an incubator until it can be released into the political sphere. It's essential, therefore, that we plan in advance to ensure that this incubator works well. The more we're able to do now, the less will need to be done later.

4

The Point of No Return: The Streets or the Commanding Heights?

At what moment does a revolution become irreversible? Many suggest that it's when the people take control of the streets. But is this so?

'The street' was and remains the principal mantra for the liberally minded Russian intelligentsia. They see their mission as bringing the masses out onto the streets. But they're generally not very good at doing this. More often than not, people react less to calls to action from the intelligentsia than they do to hidden hints that come from the authorities. This was the case in Gorbachev's time, when a split in the Central Committee of the Communist Party led to the success of the largest rally ever seen in Russian history. Sometimes, the people will take to the streets themselves, as happened at the start of the twentieth century, when the intelligentsia were left in their wake, barely able to catch up. But a far more serious problem is that, while the revolutionary leaders from the intelligentsia don't quite know what to do with the masses who've taken to the streets, those who are not from the intelligentsia do understand, but prefer not to speak out about it. That's how it's come about that, since Lenin's time, no one in Russia has been prepared to speak openly about this matter. This is no one's fault. At first, there were serious reasons for keeping quiet; later, there was simply no need to talk about it.

Why do political leaders call people out onto the streets? As discussed above, there are two main situations where this happens: for peaceful or non-peaceful protest. In this context we don't need to look at peaceful protest. If there's some hope that the dictatorship will step down under psychological pressure (for example, if the leaders have become decrepit, if there are splits among the elite, or if the regime is afraid that there'll be foreign intervention), then people are brought out onto the streets simply as a demonstration of their strength, and not as a way of overthrowing the regime. In such a situation, opposition leaders use the mob as a tool when negotiating with the representatives of the regime to discuss the terms of capitulation. But it's a completely different situation when it's clear that there will be no capitulation, and that the regime is ready to open fire on the people.

When matters have reached such a peak that the toughest measures might be needed to overthrow the authorities, the call to take to the streets becomes a call for the attack to begin; it's an open call for an uprising. Those making this call are taking on a huge responsibility. In such a situation, leaders must be prepared to take charge of the attack and to follow all the rules of revolutionary and military science. If not, then they have no right to call the people out, because such a move would simply provoke the authorities and senselessly expose people to a hailstorm of truncheons and even bullets. If you're going to lead an uprising, complete with actual street battles, it's not enough just to want people on the streets. As Lenin wrote – the only person in Russian history to have led a successful revolutionary uprising – organizing an uprising is an art and you have to learn how to do it. An uprising has to be prepared in advance. It's not something to be decided on the spur of the moment.

The reason for calling people out onto the streets in a revolutionary situation is to seize the commanding heights.

Despite how it may seem in the utopian dreams of armchair leaders, the street is not important in and of itself. It's simply a way of directing unarmed or poorly armed people at a crucial moment and bringing them together as a critical mass in one place or in several places. There needs to be a sufficient number of people in order to persuade the regime's local commanders at these previously appointed places not to take retaliatory action.

More than one hundred years ago, a revolutionary who went under the pseudonym of Postoronny, or 'the Stranger' [Lenin], rapidly dictated to his colleagues in Petrograd his advice on how to organize a revolutionary uprising. Some of his advice is now out of date, but parts of it remain relevant:

> An armed uprising is a particular form of the political struggle, and one that obeys certain laws. You need to think about them carefully. Karl Marx expressed this truth with stark clarity, when he wrote that an armed *'uprising, like a war, is an art'*.
> Marx outlined the main rules of this art thus:
>
> 1. Never *play* at an uprising; once it's begun it's essential that you know that you must *carry it to its conclusion*.
> 2. It is vital that in the right place and at the decisive moment you have *much greater numbers of forces*. If you do not then an enemy that has prepared and organized better will annihilate the rebels.
> 3. Once the uprising has begun, you must act with the greatest *decisiveness*, and most certainly go on *the attack*. 'Defence means the death of an armed uprising.'
> 4. You must try to surprise the enemy, seizing the moment when his forces are scattered.
> 5. You must achieve even small successes *every day* (you could say every hour if we're talking about actions in a single city); this way, whatever happens, you'll maintain the *moral upper hand*.

Marx summed up the lessons of armed insurrections in all revolutions with the words, 'of Danton, the greatest master of revolutionary tactics in the whole of history: courage, courage and once again, courage'.

Relating this to Russia and to October 1917, this means:

> With the combined efforts of our three main forces – the navy, the workers and military units – this means that without fail and *whatever it costs in casualties*, we must seize and hold in the first assault (a) the telephone exchange; (b) the telegraph office; (c) the railway stations; (d) the bridges.
>
> We must divide *the most reliable* elements (our 'shock troops' and the young workers, along with our best sailors) into small units in order to seize the most important objectives. Also, they must be the ones who *take part* everywhere in all the important operations, such as . . . forming the units of the very best workers with rifles and bombs to attack and surround the enemy's 'centres' (the cadet schools, the telegraph, the telephone exchange, and so on), operating under the slogan: *we may all die, but we will never give in to the enemy.*

Reading over these lines a hundred years on, when we know the outcome, we can begin to understand how important it is to acknowledge simple truths. Unfortunately, though, simplicity does not mean that it's easy to assimilate them. Let's try to consider this advice from today's point of view. We can put Marx's thoughts to one side, since these are philosophical ideas that are difficult to apply in every concrete situation. But it's worth looking further into the advice about bridges, the telegraph office, the post office, and so on. Of course, times have changed radically. The telegraph has sunk into oblivion; post has become email; and bridges have lost the significance they once had. But this is not the point.

The first thing that remains as relevant today as it was then is that it's essential to maintain the unity of political action, because, if the uprising is broken up into individual sectors, each of them can be crushed individually. Lenin needed bridges in order to maintain this unity of action, but what this really means is transport hubs, which must be isolated and immediately brought under control.

Second, and even more important, is that the rebels maintain uninterrupted communication. In the modern world, this means having control over internet and mobile phone providers, as well as protecting the means of transmitting signals (control hubs, masts, and so on). Without the coordination that this provides, the revolutionary masses quickly become just an ungovernable mob and they'll be smashed to pieces.

Third, it remains vital to control the traditional forms of mass communication: television, radio, newspapers and print. If they can't be taken over, they must at least be neutralized.

Fourth, it's very important to prevent the regime from carrying out repressions and seizing the leaders from the crowd. In order to prevent this, one of the first things to do is blockade prisons and police stations, and release any comrades who've already been arrested.

Fifth, the formation of an advance guard of units of well-trained and, if possible, armed youths remains as important as ever. They should be able at least partially to prevent the security forces from acting and provide cover for the bulk of the people. Therefore, training and arming these units both with weapons taken from the security forces and with home-made devices, such as Molotov cocktails and so forth, is also of vital importance.

Revolution is a serious business, and should never be toyed with. If you're not absolutely sure, don't try to overtake history. If you're not prepared to carry things through to the end, don't even leave your room. Don't start up any kind of movement. Just stay where you are. Don't call people out on the streets if you don't know which street to choose and where they need to go – and if you're not prepared to lead from the front. But if you do make that call, don't stop, even when there are casualties. Because if you do, there'll simply be even more casualties and, worst of all, they will have died for nothing. If you feel that you're capable of doing this, then prepare yourself. Being a revolutionary is a profession. And, as with any other profession, it doesn't tolerate amateurs. Preparing yourself means also thinking things through all the way and not being afraid of the conclusions you reach, which could be much more unpleasant than any of us might want.

5

How to Organize the New Order: Constitutional Democracy or Democracy by Decree?

An honest and principled person who is critical of the current regime in Russia is right to ask: why is moving from a bad authoritarian state to a good democratic one considered a 'problem'?

Indeed, at first glance everything looks extremely simple. After the democratic forces have triumphed (however this is accomplished), the first step must be to call a Constituent (constitutional) Assembly. Next, a new Constitution must be approved; or, at the very least, the old one must have all the unconstitutional additions removed. Then free and fair elections must be held to create the new democratic institutions. Generally speaking, this is how everything works. But the reality is somewhat more complicated. As soon as we take a closer look at this plan, it is clear that there are many practical issues to be faced. And it's much better to consider all this before we arrive at this juncture.

Common sense tells us that, even in the most favourable conditions, the three most defining actions of the new authorities – calling the Constituent Assembly, bringing the Constitution into line with democratic principles, and holding free and fair elections for the new institutions of power

– cannot be achieved in a day, or even a month. You need at least a year, probably longer. And this is in ideal circumstances; that clearly won't be the case for us.

We have to spend more time looking at these conditions, because they're hugely significant. You don't have to be a prophet to predict that, when Putin goes, many people will still retain the habit of living as they have under his regime. This means that genuine changes in life in Russia will take place far more slowly than we would wish.

Far too often, we underestimate the power of social inertia. People intrinsically hang on to whatever it is they've grown used to over many years. As a result of this, dilapidated organizations keep on working, even though they have been expected to collapse under the weight of corruption and ineffectiveness. The system shows a miraculous ability to survive against all the odds. But then, when the inertia finally exhausts itself (and it can't go on for ever), the system collapses drastically and in a way that's difficult to control. The stronger the inertia is and the longer it lasts, the greater will be the risks that need to be overcome in the transitional period.

What can any interim government expect when it attempts to simultaneously drag Russia out of its past and prepare it for the future?

1. A sharp rise in poverty due to a worsening budget deficit and limited possibilities for financial flexibility.
2. Intensification of disintegration processes and the growth of separatist sentiments.
3. Opposition and sabotage from the old elite, especially from the military and the secret services.
4. Flight of capital, directly or tangentially linked to the previous regime.
5. An increase in crime, including when the redistribution of property begins.
6. Deteriorating relations in the international sphere, since

the weakening of the situation inside the country will inevitably lead to greater pressure from outside.

In circumstances that will already be difficult, these factors could combine to create a perfect storm. Whatever good intentions the interim government may have, it will quickly find itself having to introduce emergency measures. It will have two concurrent agendas, one on top of the other, each interfering with the other. There will be the transformative agenda, aimed at creating the conditions in Russia for stable, constitutional government. And there will be the emergency agenda, that will try to maintain the political gains that have been won, while fighting off opposition from the old order and trying to bring stability to the overall socioeconomic and political situation in the country.

Politics is a never-ending process. If this process is interrupted, even if just for a few days, let alone weeks or months, then chaos will inevitably reign in the gaping chasm this brings. And we're talking here about a period of one or two years. Confusion and anarchy could produce an even worse regime for Russia than that of Putin. If we don't think about this in advance, then someone could simply seize the power that's just lying there for the taking. And whether they would then wish to share that power with anyone else is a serious question.

From a practical point of view, the success of the transformation will depend not so much on the effectiveness of the Constituent Assembly as on the competence of the government that takes over on day one of the revolution and will rule the country until a permanent government takes office following free and fair elections. This interim government must be capable of closing the gap between the start of the democratic transformation and the point when these democratic changes acquire their first institutional framework. Agreeing the goals and the tasks of the interim government is more important right now than talking about future constitutional innovations.

This can be discussed in the Constituent Assembly; but the interim government won't have time to figure things out.

The phrase 'after Putin' is a rather abstract one. 'After Putin' could happen when Putin is still alive; or it could come many years after his death. We must not assume that another Putin – or an even worse version of him – will not come to power when Putin himself goes. And this could happen several times over. Opponents of the Bolshevik regime predicted its demise nearly every year, but it continued for almost seventy years. But nothing, of course, lasts forever; everything is bound eventually to come to an end. There will come a time when civil society will be allowed to find its place in the political sphere. That will be the point at which the transitional period begins.

To some degree it doesn't matter who makes the first move, or how they do it. It could be someone from the ranks of the successors who, as Gorbachev did, will declare that 'we cannot go on living like this', and will start to gradually loosen the screws on society. It might be a 'traitor to their own class', like Yeltsin, who manages to burst through to the highest echelons of power and build 'a revolution from above'. It's not impossible that it could even be a coalition of democratic forces, that carries out 'a revolution from below' – although, in a police state such as Russia, that, for now, seems unlikely.

Those are three possible scenarios for Russia, three different fates; but whichever it is, the first act of this drama will be the same. Out of apparently nothing, a government will arise that will start to dismantle the old system that had been built strictly on the top–down principle, and it will bring those 'below' (i.e. civil society) into the political process. This government will no longer have the old 'legitimacy of tranquillity', nor will it yet have the new 'legitimacy of movement'. Its term in office will be brief, but notwithstanding this it will be faced by the most challenging and important task of all: to make the process of transformation irreversible and to save the country from breaking apart. Its mission will be accomplished when it forms a government with a new constitutional majority.

Judging by the experience of both Russia and other countries, history has shown that two years is the limit of trust that the people will give to democratic forces that begin a reform programme. After that comes a fork in the road, which is only to be expected. At that point, either power has to be transferred to a newly elected government (which will rarely have good relations with its predecessor), or the authorities can try to hold onto power with the help of revolutionary violence, overcoming opposition from the population, who are beginning to feel ever more negative about the reformers.

The second option is what happens most often; but if that path is taken then the government will likely be forced to bid farewell to any plans it had for democracy and put them aside until history's next big event. This is exactly what happened in Russia in 1993, just two years after a democratic revolution. Russia received its new Constitution on the back of the tanks that bombarded the first parliament of the new Russia. And this underlines how vital it is that, regardless of the difficulties, whatever needs to be done is accomplished in those first two years.

So the interim democratic government that comes to power after the end of the Putin regime will have a historic mission. It will have to relaunch democratic processes in Russia and lay the foundations for a permanent constitutional government – one that is legally elected. The problem, however, is that it will have to carry out this mission in the most extreme circumstances. One of the greatest challenges in a transitional period after any lengthy authoritarian rule is that it is virtually impossible to prevent the economy – and politics – from going into a nosedive. Thus, another mission for the interim government (and one that is equally important) is to forestall a societal descent into chaos.

We can be almost certain that no interim government will be able to create the conditions needed to meet high standards of democracy. Furthermore, in the initial stages it is highly likely that the old, 'rubber-stamp' institutions, such as the State Duma and the Federation Council, will have to be dismantled. A particularly tricky question will be what to do with the courts. Here, contradictions arise between, first, the irremovability and independence of judges; second, the need to carry out a radical purge of the corrupt personnel of the old regime; and, third, the rights of offenders, suspects and victims. At the same time, the government must maintain a course of democratization, not allowing for any temporary restrictions to become permanent; ensuring that a Constituent Assembly is called and carries out real work; that a new Constitution is adopted; and that free and fair elections are held.

What sort of government will be needed to make progress along these divergent paths? In an ideal world, it will be a government of national unity that includes representatives of various political forces and is based on a consensus with civil society. Something along the lines of an 'opposition coordinating council' that had been granted power. However, in real life such an ideal is virtually impossible to achieve. Initially, when the movement begins, there simply won't be fully formed political forces in the country that can be relied on and that genuinely reflect civil society. In their place, we will have a plethora of political groups whose aims are unclear and whose legitimacy is dubious. Then, even if there were someone who wanted to cobble together such a political kaleidoscope as the foundation for an interim government, nothing would come of it (as we saw with the 'coordinating council' that was formed in 2012). Finally, whoever it is that takes power at the start will have to be highly motivated to invite others to share power. So far, no one in Russia has been magnanimous enough to do that. It would be extraordinary to expect that to happen in the future.

Therefore, it's highly unlikely that an interim government made up of a coalition of revolutionary forces could be formed that would represent a significant segment of civil society

– however much we might wish for this to happen. It's far more likely that power will lie in the hands of a single political force: either the reformers from above, or the revolutionaries from below. And neither force will have the time or the desire to spread its power around.

In its turn, this will seriously increase the risk that the inevitable temporary dictatorship of the revolution will become a long-term project. So what can be done to prevent the process of building a democracy and moving the country onto a constitutional track from stalling?

Common sense suggests that, in order to succeed, some kind of balance of forces is needed as a counterweight to the work of the interim government. But where can such a counterbalance be found? Nearly all the purely 'decorative' representative institutions of the old authorities have been discredited or have long outlived their usefulness. What's more, when the revolutionary changes begin, members of these institutions will, on the whole, be against the revolution and thus not in a position to give any help at all. And it's likely that, given their current state, it will be necessary to suspend the State Duma and the Federation Council altogether. But it will also be impossible to hold elections quickly for the new representative bodies. This will take months, at best, during which time every day will be precious.

However strange it may seem, it's the present regime that has given us a possible solution. In the rush to guarantee their leader a permanent place in power, they created, among other things, a quasi-representative body, the State Council, and even gave it legal standing via the Constitution. The purpose of this institution was to put the brakes on any changes. But if the personnel there were to be changed, and people were selected according to different principles, this counterrevolutionary organization would become a revolutionary one.

In practice, the State Council could be reformed almost instantaneously if the interim government were to fill it with representatives from civil society and the regions. For the transitional period, it could be the political centre that keeps the authorities in check, and it could become the temporary emergency legislative body and the oversight organization for the interim government. Furthermore, it would allow for a certain constitutional continuity between the old authorities and the new. The State Council could issue temporary decrees that would lay the normative and legal foundation for the work of the government in the period of transition.

The principles on which the State Council will be formed is the subject of a lengthy, separate discussion, that can really be had only when the general outlines of the transition are known. But there can be no doubt about one thing: if the transition is too draconian, then the only legitimate foundation for the formation of the State Council will be regional representation, since the legitimacy of all the other institutions of power will be in doubt. In this case, the State Council will be made up of authorized representatives of the regions, probably elected or appointed by the local legislative assemblies. It will also be clear that, for the State Council to work quickly and effectively, it should create a smaller governing body, operating on a permanent basis.

Thus, the interim government and the State Council should work in tandem, enabling the system of power to operate for a long enough period to call a Constituent Assembly, give it a chance to do its work, introduce a new Constitution and electoral laws, and also run free and fair elections for the new institutions as defined by the Constitution. This must not take any longer than two years. If it does, then Russian history will simply enter yet another round of totalitarianism.

6

How to Bring an End to the War: Fight to a Victorious Outcome, Capitulate, or Seek a Compromise?

This chapter was written almost a year before Russia unleashed the greatest geopolitical disaster of the past one hundred years: the war against Ukraine. Strange as it may seem, the chapter hardly needed editing.

The interim government that will have to dismantle the regime will be faced by a mountain of problems. But it's already clear that the greatest of these will be to bring an end to the war with Ukraine – in reality with the West – into which Putin's regime has dragged Russia.

The war with Ukraine is simply the tip of the iceberg. Beneath it and at its core is the global confrontation with the West, conducted wherever the regime can do so. Militarism is the very essence of Putin's regime. The only way in which it can stabilize itself internally is to conduct constant wars against imaginary enemies, both internal and external. War is the price to be paid for corruption. This gang of corrupt opportunists who seized and usurped power in Russia at the start of the century cannot hold onto their positions without a war, and they're carrying out their latest one to try to defend the narrow interests of their clans.

Russia has been in a cold war situation with the West from

the moment that Putin delivered his speech at Munich in 2007. And in February 2022, this war became a hot war. For now, it's being waged on the territory of Ukraine. But let's not deceive ourselves. The assault on Ukraine is simply the first of a number of predetermined goals. This war that the Kremlin desperately needs in order to stabilize and maintain its fascist regime is imperialist, criminal and, of course, unjust. But as well as all the grief and suffering that it's bringing to the Ukrainian people, not to mention all the grief that it's bringing to the families of the Russian soldiers who are dying and being wounded in this criminal war that no one needs – as well as all this, it's draining Russia of the resources that are essential for its development. This war is destroying the future of Russia itself. It is the principal obstacle preventing the formation of an alternative strategy for the country's development. Unless this crazy and exhausting war is brought to an end, there is no hope of moving to a constructive, creative and socially oriented agenda. The problem is that bringing an end to this war is going to be far more difficult than launching it was. So any interim government will be faced with a very serious challenge in the transitional period. This is also because ending the war in a careless and irresponsible way is no less dangerous politically than continuing it.

In theory, there are only three ways to end a war: victory, surrender, or some kind of compromise. Trying to win the current war with Ukraine would be a criminal and immoral act. Furthermore, if we understand that the real purpose of this war and its ultimate goal is the defeat of the West, then we can see that it's also a utopian ideal. If the regime could not achieve this at the peak of its powers, then it will be even more impossible for an interim government to achieve this in the conditions of economic downturn and political instability that will follow in the transitional period. So in reality there are just two options that can be considered: unconditional surrender, or a search for more or less acceptable conditions for peace.

But the problem is that after all that the Putin regime has done, it will be extremely difficult to try to stipulate any such conditions.

Having unleashed the war, Putin has effectively taken off the table any question concerning 'the Russian world' [the so-called *russky mir* – Tr.]. The whole concept of 'the Russian world' is now associated only with aggression. What's more, Moscow can no longer play the role of being at its heart. We have to recognize clearly and decisively the consequences of what has happened, and not hide our heads in the sand like ostriches. Putin has taken Russian culture and Russian civilization from the global level and turned it into something merely regional. This phase transition is likely to prove permanent, and history won't revise that opinion. Against this general background, a separate issue is that Russian Orthodoxy has been turned into a regional, even a local, religion, that no longer has the right to preach morality to the world or lay claim to being 'the Third Rome'. This is the world in which we will be living, and whether Putin is there or not is irrelevant. Even if Putin departs the scene, none of this grandeur will return.

But there are even more serious consequences. Having witnessed Putin's aggression, very many countries – notably nearly all of Russia's immediate neighbours – will reckon that their safety can be guaranteed only by the dismemberment of Russia. The threat of the collapse of Russia is the principal result of Putin's war that the interim government will have to deal with. And this government is going to have very little time at its disposal. The only way that Russia can be maintained as a single, sovereign state is for the government to be proactive in all directions. The first thing it will have to do is make peace with all the parties that have been drawn into this conflict; it will then need to carry out a programme of federalization. Federalization is a subject for a separate discussion, but the question of peace has to be discussed here and now.

There's a very simplistic view of this problem that's popular among the liberal opposition – namely, that the answer
is merely to reverse everything that Putin's done. So: Putin
started the war in Ukraine, therefore we must stop it immediately. Putin put his medium-range missiles on high alert in
violation of a treaty: they must be destroyed. Putin built military bases in Africa: they must be closed down and the troops
sent back to Russia. And so on.

I wrote the first draft of this book before the war. In it, I considered at this point possible solutions using as an example the
problem of Crimea. But the war has changed all that. Today
the confrontation has created such a rift in Russian society, and
the propaganda and mobilization have had such a profound
effect upon people's consciousness, that it's now impossible to
imagine any gradual, long-drawn-out solutions. In the present,
specific case, this makes the situation very straightforward: a
genuine change of regime is now possible only in the event of
a military defeat. This means that the Crimea problem, like the
wider problem of ending the war, can be solved only by way of
a peace treaty. For now, I find it very difficult to imagine that
Ukraine would be prepared to sign such a treaty unless it is
granted the full restoration of sovereignty over the territories
that were within its internationally recognized borders in 1991.
Of course, anything is possible, but unless Putin's regime suf-
fers a military defeat, it won't be replaced any time soon.

A military defeat would signal the end of the war, and
one way or another it would resolve the issue of the annexed
territories. But the peace treaty itself would not mean that
everything would return to the way it was before the war. The
division between Russians and Ukrainians and between Russia
and Europe is now vast, and no government is going to be able
to heal this rift in the short term, least of all an interim government that doesn't enjoy significant legitimacy or sufficient
reserves of time or trust. The inevitable economic and political
crisis that will result from a military defeat and the dramatic

collapse of the economy will leave the interim government in a position whereby it will have to solve the many ongoing problems using all the resources at its disposal; or else it will simply collapse, leaving the way clear for radical nationalist groups and other populists. At the same time, the Ukrainian government will have to demand just as firmly the resources to rebuild their country; and there will be no simple answer to how Russia should act here. Unfortunately, yet totally justifiably, today we can say with certainty that all the assets that have been seized – some 300 billion dollars, including the foreign assets of Putin's oligarchs – should go to repair the damage caused as a result of the war. But I shall be extremely surprised if this satisfies Ukraine. At the same time, the inhabitants of Tatarstan and the Russian Far East, of Voronezh and the Trans-Baikal Region, are hardly likely to vote for increasing their own impoverishment and not that of Putin's oligarchs.

Someone is bound to say, 'let's discuss everything'. Okay. But, first, discussion takes time – and time is going to be in short supply. And second, discussing the issues doesn't mean reaching agreement on them. Right now, we don't know what the position of the other side will be. And given everything that's happened under Putin between Russia and Ukraine – and, more widely, between Russia and the West – there is not likely to be much appetite on the other side to seek a compromise. It's more likely that Russia will find itself up against strong pressure and with very little bargaining power. At least, this is what the experience of the 1990s tells us. No one proposed a 'Marshall Plan' for Russia then, and it's highly unlikely that anyone will suggest one now. This all leads to the idea that the restoration of justice, which may appear to be a logical step, will be of benefit to some, while others will regard it as shocking and an injustice.

Now let's look at the second part of the question of restitution: the political one. Is this likely to be popular in Russian society, even in that section of society that is prepared to support an interim government in its efforts to dismantle the Putin regime? Probably not. Especially if the humanitarian consequences of swift and unconditional restitution become immediately obvious. It seems inevitable that this will lead to a sharp rise in discontent, something that reactionary forces will quickly try to use to their advantage. If this is so, the interim government won't last more than a few months. Politics is the art of the possible. Extricating ourselves so easily from Putin's war with the West – acknowledging that we were wrong and trying to return everything to the way it was – will, most likely, not be possible.

Many of those who believe in simple solutions refer to the Peace of Brest-Litovsk, which the Bolsheviks signed with Germany when Russia withdrew from the First World War. They suggest that, after the dismantling of the regime has begun, Russia should conclude similar agreements with all those against whom Putin has been waging war. But the Peace of Brest-Litovsk is a bad example to choose. The Bolsheviks acted in conditions of an extreme *force majeure*, under which, had they taken any other decision, they would simply have lost power. And they were ready to break all the terms of the agreement at the first opportunity, which is exactly what they did after just a few months when a revolution took place in Germany. Taking advantage of the confusion this caused, the Moscow government seized back everything they had given away, including wiping out Ukraine's independence that had been accepted on the fringes of the Brest-Litovsk agreements. Had it not been for the revolution in Germany, the Bolsheviks' gamble may have had a completely different outcome.

When all things are considered, the only possible scenario will be to move forwards, not backwards. Naturally, it calls for courage to admit one's mistakes and call a spade a spade, including acknowledging crimes as crimes. Those who committed these crimes must bear full responsibility for them and accept the consequences. But the way out of this situation must be found in keeping with the new reality as things are now. This is no simple task. In each specific case a balance must be sought between restoring the old justice and creating a new injustice; between acknowledging what is politically essential and turning away from what is politically impossible.

A likely compromise for the period of transition will be the very admission of the existence of a problem and a willingness to resolve it.

Rejecting Putin's legacy does not mean, unfortunately, that we can simply ignore it. The war represents the new reality, and the way out of it must be well organized and properly thought through. For this to happen, certain important points must be noted, namely:

1. Old problems can never be solved simply by creating new ones.
2. What is politically desirable must be separated from what is politically possible.
3. It must be clearly understood where the interests of Putin's regime end and where Russia's national interests begin; solving the problem of de-Putinization must not damage Russia's national interests.
4. Each point should be approached separately, noting the unique difficulties of each one; there should not be a rush to find a universal, standard solution.
5. We must be prepared to recognize that historically proven ways of solving many problems simply don't exist; they will have to be worked out afresh.
6. Time and political will are needed in order to solve many problems.

7

How to Defeat an Internal Counterrevolution: Remove the Old Guard, or Try to Correct Them?

Russia went through difficult times on its way back to its Soviet past. It has already passed the point of no return. There's no turning back. The chain of events was thus:

- Yeltsin pushed forward Putin as his successor;
- Putin gradually took over total power;
- there were creeping counter-reforms;
- the return (in effect) of state control over the economy, albeit indirectly – it's not so much 'the state' as it is 'the mafia' (in other words, the situation is worse than in Soviet times).

Taken together, this means that more than a quarter of a century after Gorbachev's perestroika, Russia has not only returned to the starting point of his reforms, but in many ways has gone back to a time many decades before that.

This Soviet restoration poses the practical question about the strength of the reactionaries who are trying to extinguish any kind of reform or revolution and reinstate themselves in power. Putin and his closest circle are representatives of the second and third levels of the Soviet *nomenklatura* (those at the highest level, as a rule, lose the most and are no longer in a position to reinstate themselves to their previous positions). These people from the second and third levels slipped into the background, yet were waiting there, ready to carry out an ambush. When the opportunity arose, they came to the fore and tried to turn back the clock to restore the old values and ways of ruling, which they remembered well from their youth. Naturally, they did this by adapting to contemporary conditions, which meant first and foremost that they considered it essential to make themselves as rich as possible.

This is not a unique situation, of course. When an interim government comes to power, forces linked to the old regime never disappear instantaneously from the face of the earth. Some of them will be eased out, but many will remain in place. And they won't just remain in place; they'll stay there with all their money, their retinues, and the old connections that they've built up, along with their economic and social capital. They – or, to be more precise, already these second- and third-level officials – will also be awaiting the opportunity to re-establish themselves in their previous positions. This is why any new group that comes to power always has to try to avoid being crushed by representatives of the old regime. But how can they achieve this? How do they define the boundaries that are so essential for their political defence? How do they avoid going too far in defending themselves against the old terror without giving rise to a new terror? Where do you draw the line of reasonable sufficiency when it comes to suppressing an internal counterrevolution?

These are the questions that many people are struggling with today, not in an abstract sense but precisely as they consider recent experience. When they examine closely the 1990s, people want to understand what it was that they missed. What mistakes were made that allowed the Soviet Union to return? By far the most popular answer is that it's because there was failure to conduct a 'lustration' – a purge of the old guard.

When we look at today's political situation we could argue that not conducting a lustration was undoubtedly a mistake. But I wouldn't jump to this conclusion.

In the broadest sense of the term, lustration is the disenfranchisement of representatives of the old elite. How widely this reaches can vary, both in terms of the people affected and the rights that are taken away from them. If we're talking about Russia, then probably the most wide-ranging lustration was undertaken by the Bolsheviks after the Revolution. They used repressive measures against millions of people who fell into the category of the so-called 'privileged classes' of the old Russia (the nobility, members of the clergy, army officers, the kulaks and others). A significant percentage of them were repressed in various ways or even killed, while millions of others were denied the right to take part in various activities, professions were closed off to them, their children were deprived of the possibility to be educated, and so on.

But this is an extreme example. After the 'velvet revolutions' in Europe, 'velvet lustrations' became fashionable. They were on a much smaller scale and were a lot more gentle in terms of the pressure they put on the old elite. Whole social classes were no longer included among those who were lustrated. Now it was more about individuals who directly cooperated with the regime or who occupied specific positions in its hierarchy. These could have been officials (in the first instance, of course, members of the law-enforcement bodies or the special services), judges, secret agents or other similar categories. The lists of these people differed depending on the country, but the general principle was the same: a change from class-based repression to specific professional or political categories.

Naturally, in modern Russia you won't find many people who would want to repeat the 'Red Terror'. But in terms of milder restrictions, such as those applied in Eastern Europe or certain countries of the post-Soviet space, there tends to be a different opinion. A significant proportion of the liberally minded intelligentsia today would welcome such an approach. People look to the past and say: 'We didn't do this in the 1990s – and look what happened!' But before answering the question as to whether or not this should be done, it would be sensible to ask whether in principle it would be possible to do this in Russia. And the answer to this question is not as simple as it may seem.

A so-called 'mild lustration' would principally aim to break the chain of automatic self-perpetuation of the *nomenklatura* – a somewhat closed circle of professional bureaucrats who amazingly manage to retain their positions inside any power set-up following a revolution. There are many examples of this; and they all show that – in the countries of the former USSR at least – no purge is going to solve this issue.

Let's start with the Bolsheviks themselves. Already at the beginning of the 1920s, just three years after the Revolution and the start of the 'Red Terror', Lenin was complaining in letters to his colleagues that the Bolsheviks had been unable to solve the problem of clearing out the representatives of the old tsarist state apparatus. He moaned that they represented the overwhelming majority of Soviet state officials; that the new state apparatus was even bigger than the old one had been; and that it was suffering from every kind of bureaucratic illness. To be fair, it should be noted that, in the end, the Bolsheviks did manage to overcome the political opposition of the old elites; but this was mainly by terror rather than by measures that could, in a narrower sense of the word, be described as 'lustration'.

The most recent experience of lustration in Ukraine can also hardly be called encouraging. First, it turned out that efforts to use legislation to sack officials were, in practice, beset with massive and often insurmountable difficulties. Then, it turned out that once all those who needed to be removed were gone, the new authorities found that they had no one available to fill key posts. It is this factor that runs through all the unsuccessful attempts at lustration across the whole post-Soviet space.

This is in contrast to the relatively positive experience of this method in the countries of Eastern Europe.

Russia's problem (and, indeed, that of many other post-Soviet states) is that the political class, and indeed the entire cultural layer in the country, is not very big. As a result, the substitutes' bench for filling these posts in any future adminis-tration is very small. There simply isn't anywhere to find a large number of judges, prosecutors or police, let alone bankers, financial inspectors and so on. And the further you go, the more difficult it is, because the work of the state apparatus becomes ever more complicated, and the tasks allocated to it ever greater. In other words, lustration is all well and good in theory, but it rarely works in practice. It even became an insoluble problem for the Bolsheviks, despite their conviction that any cook would be capable of running the country. It ended up with the cooks becoming the bosses, but under them it was still basically the old specialists doing the work. In real-ity, we need to find a different solution besides lustration.

And there is a solution. It turns out that, when placed in completely different circumstances, the very same people are capable of showing completely different results. The task should be to change not the people, but the system that defines the limits of their behaviour. This task can be split into two separate areas: removing the 'star pupils' from the system and cutting out unacceptable social and political work practices.

As accumulated experience has shown, trying to disenfran-chise social and professional groups when there is no one else who can take their place simply makes the situation even more complicated. One way or another, representatives of these groups still manage to worm their way into the new social structure, causing serious moral and political damage to soci-ety. A useful method here may be to take a more personalized approach, which would help at least for a time to exclude the more odious characters from this infrastructure. We are, of course, not including here those against whom there is clear evidence for bringing legal charges in connection with particularly serious crimes. Such individuals must be brought before the courts, in accordance with all the constitutional guarantees.

We are instead talking about people who are not suspected of carrying out particularly dangerous crimes themselves, but who were key figures in facilitating the work of the criminal regime – such as those who sponsored the regime, who created its propaganda, who were in charge of crucial sections of the apparatus of repression. Bringing them all to justice would be costly, even if it were possible; but allowing them to continue to engage in political activity would be dangerous. One solution could be to apply personal and targeted sanctions, which are, in any case, fairer than lustration based solely on professional or social grounds. Some sort of 'internal Magnitsky Act' could be used that would allow for the regime's 'star pupils' to be excluded from the social infrastructure, albeit only for a limited period of time.

Naturally, though, this is not enough. If you simply exclude the star pupils, then pretty quickly the second- and third-tier officials will be striving to move up the ladder. Therefore, a ban on the preaching of unacceptable social and political actions, which are inextricably linked to mass violations of human rights and freedoms, should be added to measures designed to combat internal counterrevolution. The processes of de-communization and de-Stalinization showed specifically the desire to do this. Many consider that these were two more opportunities that were missed in the 1990s. This is partly true; but it's not as simple as that.

In the 1990s, it was thought that de-communization meant first and foremost outlawing the activities of the Communist Party. Yet this was a genuine political force that, to this day, is still supported by millions of people. Trying to do this inevitably divided society. Exactly the same thing would happen today, and it's unlikely that it would succeed.

The fact is, terror is not an essential element in the basic idea of Communism. It's just one of the possible ways in which it can develop, and one that, unfortunately, became the reality in Russia. Rather than splitting society by just outlawing labels, it's important to firmly suppress attempts to spread and popularize the practices that are hidden behind those labels. When we're talking about Communist ideas, this means roughly the following: preventing attempts to justify the Great Terror (and terror in general), to preach the forcible expropriation of property, and to preach genocide based on social or ethnic grounds; in other words, everything that went to make up the dark pages of Russian history in the twentieth century. In some senses this is similar to the Chinese approach to de-Maoization. Without actually attacking the figure of Mao himself (indeed, it's still difficult for them to make an unambiguous assessment of him as a national leader), the Chinese Communist Party had to condemn very severely the extremes of the Maoist terror, including the so-called Cultural Revolution and the twists and turns in the battle against private property.

So it's essential to strike a balance. On the one hand, we have to defend the new authorities and not allow for yet another return to the previous regime; but at the same time, we also have to avoid a split in society and a civil war, which would, in any case, lead to the return of the regime, albeit somewhat later. Lustration is not a dogma, but a general idea; and how it's done has to be in accordance with the situation at a given time and place. Lustration for its own sake doesn't lead to anything positive, nor does it protect you from a counterrevolution.

8

How to Control the Man with a Gun: A Task for the Party or for the Secret Services?

Even in politically stable times, the work of both genuine and even 'rubber-stamp' institutions can hide the violent nature of any state. But its true nature is always present. A state is a complicated and multifunctional institution, but, at the end of the day, it still remains a machine for violence. To be more precise, it's a machine for legitimized violence, since it's only this legitimacy that differentiates the state from just any armed group that enforces its will on those around it using violent means. But when an era of change replaces that political stability, and when the old way of life collapses but has yet to be replaced by something new, the violent nature of state power comes to the fore.

Because of this, an enormous problem faces any interim government in the very first days of its existence: how does it control the man with a gun, or, as we're used to saying these days, the *siloviki*? Today, they're part of an enclosed system, where they all keep a beady eye on each other, and Putin himself watches them all constantly like a hawk. But once Putin goes, the closed circle will break, and dozens, if not hundreds, of scattered armed and organized groups will be left to their own devices. They might recognize the authority of the interim government, or they might place themselves on the side of the reactionaries; or they may even try to take power themselves, although this last one is unlikely as there's never been a tradition in Russia of this happening.

If events turn out this way, there will inevitably be a host of negative consequences, the most serious of which could be a counterrevolutionary uprising or a slide into civil war with the potential for the state to split apart. Thus, from the first moment it becomes a task of the greatest urgency for the interim government to ensure that the senior and middle-ranking commanders in law enforcement and the military take their political orders from them. It's no less than a matter of life or death. However well set up is the system of democratic institutions, it would take only the slightest glitch for this question to become most acute. All we need to do is look back to the day in Washington when Trump's supporters stormed the Capitol building and remember how great were the efforts of both sides in the democratic USA to liaise with the leadership of the Department of Defense and the Chiefs of Staff when they were deciding whether or not to call out the National Guard.

This question of having control over the man with a gun has been the backdrop to every change of totalitarian leader, including in the USSR, with its well-established system of ideological inheritance of power. The success of the coup against Lavrenty Beria in 1953 was greatly helped by the army remaining loyal to the Party and the Soviet leadership represented by Nikita Khrushchev and Georgy Malenkov. Khrushchev's fall from power nine years later was in no small way aided by his being betrayed by the then leadership of the KGB, which supported Leonid Brezhnev, who was already heavily backed by the army. A significant factor that assisted Mikhail Gorbachev when he came to power in 1985 was that he was seen as the protégé of the former head of the KGB, Yury Andropov. In his early days this guaranteed the loyalty of the KGB leadership, helped by the neutral position adopted by senior army officers.

The refusal of the KGB's Group Alpha to storm the parliament building in August 1991 was the death knell for the plans of the State Committee for the State of Emergency – the GKChP – to turn the clock back to hard-line Communism. One way or another, any change of power inevitably involves the question of who controls the men with the guns. You won't find this question widely discussed in text books about democracy, but there isn't a single democracy in the world that would have existed if, in each instance, this matter hadn't been decided beforehand.

In Russia, it is decided in accordance with its centuries-old traditions and way of life. As a rule, this involves preventative violence, sometimes very clearly displayed, at others more behind the scenes. In the intense phase of the conflict in 1953, Beria and his closest supporters were effectively eliminated with no investigation and no trial. The situation with the GKChP passed off without bloodshed; after being arrested and imprisoned briefly, those who took part in the coup attempt were released and even given the chance to take part in the new Russia's political life. If the forces are fortuitously aligned, the issue can be settled by simply replacing the old leadership with a new, more loyal one. But it can be difficult to guarantee such an alignment.

In any case, within a matter of hours of its being in power, the interim government will have to carry out a vote of confidence among the *siloviki*, demanding from them full recognition of the government's legitimacy. If such recognition is forthcoming, the problem is removed and it allows time for a gradual strengthening of political control over the law-enforcement agencies and the military (that is, the *siloviki*). However, should there be any doubt expressed, or, worse still, any opposition, the interim government has to take tough action, even physically neutralizing those who refuse to recognize its authority (in the best case, this would be by carrying out arrests; but even this may prove to be difficult). All of this is possible, though;

it's all been done many times throughout history, and there is no other way of accomplishing this. Either the new authorities show everybody who's boss right from the start, or they'll be destroyed – if not immediately, then soon afterwards. Politics is a cruel business, and if you don't acknowledge this then you're simply not telling it as it is. I believe that this is unacceptable, because unswerving honesty must be the basis of the new politics.

So, in the shortest possible period of time, the new authorities must bring the law-enforcement agencies and the military under their control. If they are incapable of doing this, then they don't hold power. And there's no point in trying to work out in advance exactly how to do this: there are no ready-made recipes for it.

But there's another important subject. Using force to control a man with a gun is not a problem. The problem arises with how to put a stop to this. Who makes the decision about the removal of the old *siloviki* and how it is carried out? Who makes the decision about the appointment of the new *siloviki*? Should it be the new leader, who is now head of the interim government? That would mean that he would become Russia's new dictator. First, because if he's responsible for blood being shed (if it is indeed shed), then there's no way back. And second, because any new people whom he personally appoints will be beholden to him alone in the future.

We've already seen an example of this happen with Boris Yeltsin in 1993. First there was an unsuccessful coup attempt and Yeltsin showed that he could be tough (at least from the point of view of the technology of the struggle for power), not allowing the seat of power to be dragged out from under him and suppressing the uprising of the people in the White House. As a result, he personally filled all the key posts with those who were beholden to him. It then turned out that he didn't have to do anything else. Having put his own people in all the law-enforcement agencies and the military, he no longer needed to engage in politics and the art of compromise – but without this, genuine politics no longer exists. After 1993 Yeltsin just pretended to play at politics, holding onto power mainly by strong-arm methods. And then he passed on the baton to someone who could do this even better.

How can we avoid this trap? How do we guarantee the success of the revolution without slipping back into the old ways? It seems to me that one possible way of doing this is to delegate decisions to do with sanctions on the *siloviki* to a specially created structure that is formally separate from the interim government. Earlier, I touched on the question of how a State Council, formed on a mixed regional and party principle, could assume a legislative and judicial function for a short time were there to be a temporary breakdown in the work of the representative and judicial authorities. Inside this State Council something akin to a military commission could be set up, which would be a special emergency body granted the authority to make decisions about the removal and appointment of the leaders of the law-enforcement agencies and the military on the recommendation of the interim government and in the interests of the defence of the new authorities.

Such a separation of powers could prove to be a workable and useful idea and would prevent too much power ending up in the hands of the head of the interim government – power that he could, as a result, use not for society's interests but for his own. No revolution passes off without the use of violence in a more or less mild form. But the use of force can rapidly lead society into a new authoritarian cycle. This vicious circle has to be stopped, or else the terror will never end. One way to do this, in my opinion, is that right from the start there should be an agreement that the new authorities will seek to delegate the process of taking decisions about the implementation of repressive measures.

This is the main thing. The details may vary, and exactly what they are can be agreed upon later. I discussed one option above:

decisions should be taken by a special commission of the State Council about the leadership of the law-enforcement agencies and the military on the recommendation of the interim government. This is a temporary organizational structure, but one from which the fully fledged constitutional separation of power should eventually emerge. But if no measures are taken to achieve this, all that will come of it will be violence and terror under new slogans.

9

How to Create a Civil Service: Employ Our Own Weak Staff or the Best from Abroad?

There is one reform that should be started immediately: administrative reform. It might seem that, in the transitional period, the interim government will have many other urgent tasks to tackle. But if you're going to deal with something, you must have well-working tools with which to do it. If the government doesn't have a properly functioning state apparatus at its disposal, if all its instructions simply sink into a bureaucratic quagmire, then it won't be able to achieve anything.

The quality of the state apparatus of a future government seems of secondary importance – until the future arrives. This may be why, today, this question lies on the fringes of the public's attention. But it's well known that, after any change of power, this quickly becomes one of the most important issues – yet by then it's too late to discuss it. What tends to happen is that the new authorities are forced to rush to the old state apparatus for help. In order to avoid this, it makes sense to agree on the basic approaches to the problem ahead of time.

Few people among the opposition worry about the effectiveness of the state apparatus because the thought prevails among them that there are only two problems with power in

Russia: the lack of democracy, and corruption. Many of them honestly suggest that all you have to do is solve even just one of these issues and everything else will fall into order behind it. The Russian opposition seems to believe in the old Russian tradition of relying on luck when it comes to state-building: once democracy prevails, corruption will simply disappear, and everything else will fall into place.

It's not difficult to see where such an idea comes from. In a situation where the main task for the opposition is the battle against an authoritarian regime – and, what's more, one that is degenerating into neo-totalitarianism – it seems only natural that the principal item on the agenda should be democratization. And to some extent, this is true. But something that doesn't seem so important today will become one of the biggest headaches tomorrow, when the interim government starts to carry out its functions. The new authorities' ability to survive and demonstrate their competitive advantage over the old government will depend also on how well they are able to show that they can quickly and effectively construct a new state apparatus.

Unfortunately, democratization in itself doesn't solve the problem of effective state administration. This depends more on the quality of the new bureaucracy. And democratization can actually often complicate the solution to this problem. Contrary to what many people think, democratization and improving the efficiency of the state apparatus are not only separate tasks, but ones that can actually interfere with one another. When democratization takes place rapidly and spontaneously, discipline can slacken, unbalancing the institutions of state. This isn't surprising. But it can be very dangerous if, as the new government is taking its first steps, it doesn't move to restore discipline and generally raise the effectiveness of the bureaucratic system. If democracy isn't based on a properly functioning state apparatus, then it will simply discredit the very idea of democracy itself.

Despite what many people think, the unprecedented scope of corruption in Russia doesn't represent an insurmountable barrier to building an efficient, modern civil service. On the contrary, starting to create a properly functioning civil service would be the first step to overcoming corruption in Russia. Of course, it's impossible to wipe out corruption completely in any country. We can see how widespread it is in the West – and, what's more, how actively the Putin regime makes use of this to further its influence. But it's well within the capabilities of the interim government to bring down the extreme levels of corruption that we see in Russia today. So corruption shouldn't be presented as either an unassailable obstacle or the main problem.

Corruption in Russia today has been artificially created and imposed by the current authorities and supported by political means. If it's not encouraged externally, then it will shrink significantly and relatively quickly. The point is not that officials are inclined to take bribes, but that, instead of battling against this inevitable phenomenon, the current regime relies on exploiting and cultivating corruption. In modern Russia it's simply impossible not to take and give bribes, and anyone who doesn't do this becomes doubly dangerous for the authorities. Corruption oils the wheels of Putin's terror machine. Without it, this sort of state structure is incapable of operating. Remove the political motivation, stop imposing corruption from above as a way of controlling the elites, and you'll see how the infamous and unsurpassable Russian corruption rapidly decreases to average world levels. Of course, it won't disappear entirely, just as it hasn't disappeared in America or in Europe, despite all the achievements of Western civilization. But it will become a controlled evil, rather than a tool of control. I've noticed that if corruption consumes more than 2 per cent of a state budget, it becomes a threat to the very existence of that state. In such a case, it's not corruption itself that has to be fought, but the system of control that has made it so huge, because if it's not specially stimulated, then it simply can't grow this big all by itself.

I can point to my own experience at YUKOS. When our team joined the company, every level of management was eaten up by corruption. This was because it was being imposed from the very top. When the company passed into the hands of a private owner who wasn't interested in stealing from himself, the natural motivation to spread corruption disappeared. The rest was a matter of technology, which was pretty basic. Each employee was given a proposition that was hard to refuse: either you stop stealing and earn a decent salary, or you're out and, in the worst cases, legal action may be taken. If this isn't just a game, but actual policy, everything is solved very quickly. It took us less than two years. This is why I don't see corruption as an insurmountable challenge. But on the other hand, solving it doesn't deal with the issue of competent management. An idiot who isn't corrupt but is lazy can sometimes be more dangerous than a bright spark who's corrupt.

From the very first days it will be essential to start creating the state structures as an independent task, unconnected with the work of building democracy or the battle against corruption. But in Russia there's an extra, cultural factor that complicates things in trying to achieve this: namely, the deep-rooted tradition of seeing any government official just as a lazy thief, and one whose work could be done by anyone at all. What makes it worse is that not only is this impression widespread among the general population, but it's shared also by a significant part of the educated urban population and the democratically inclined intelligentsia. This is a real impediment when it comes to considering the work of state-building to be worth taking seriously.

This attitude to government officials found its most grotesque form in the well-known Bolshevik view that any cook would and should run the state. Just a couple of years after the Revolution, though, Lenin was complaining that the

government had had to recall to its service most of the bureaucrats who had earlier been dismissed. Each had to be watched
over by a commissar. On a rather smaller scale, this happened
again at the start of the 1990s. After Gorbachev's and Yeltsin's
perestroika, most of the Soviet *nomenklatura* found themselves a place inside the new governmental structures. This
was inevitable. You can't just pluck managers out of thin air, or
create them from scratch. When no others are available, you
have to use those you already have, however unpleasant this
may be.

This constant negative attitude to officialdom in Russia came
about because for centuries managing people wasn't seen as an
art or a profession. And yet it's one of the most complicated
areas of professional activity. It needs lengthy and complicated
training, and very serious qualifications and skills that come
only with long experience. The philosopher Max Weber considered the training of an effective official to be one of the most
complicated tasks there is, and one that costs society more than
anything else. He suggested that modern officialdom in Europe
came about as a by-product of the development of capitalism,
with its complex culture of management. Overcoming Russian
traditions in this area together with the creation of a professional and modern civil service should be seen by the interim
government as the starting point for working out the general
approach to the formation of a civil service in the new Russia.

To pause briefly on the most general principles that should
guide the interim government in resolving this issue, I would
underline four points:

1. Change the attitude to government service and officialdom
   as a social class. Contempt for the bureaucracy (which
   is understandable and easy to explain, and which even
   becomes hatred), should be replaced by a constructive and
   respectful approach. Officials and civil servants should be
   seen by society as people who are carrying out an essential

role. If this isn't the case, then the other side of the same coin is impossible to fulfil: people should be able to expect a high standard of work, and accountability, from officials.

2. Separate the civil service from politics. The civil service should be professional and apolitical. Politicians come and go, but this shouldn't affect the civil service. The civil service should operate according to its own internal statutes and follow its own internal code of conduct, in accordance with which a career path should depend entirely on professional qualities, and not on whether someone supports one political opinion or another. Officials should be chosen to serve predominantly on the basis of the results of open competition, and should be selected for promotion thanks to their achievements, also decided predominantly on the basis of competition. In brief, a civil service has to be created from virtually nothing in Russia, and, as a separate institution of government, it should be capable of working with any political leadership.

3. Administrative and commercial (service) activity should be separated. The experience of successful civil services around the world shows that the more functions that the state outsources to commercial and non-commercial organizations, the more effectively the bureaucracy works. The ultimate aim of this is as much as possible to free up state employees from serving the public, so that they can concentrate on carrying out regulatory and oversight functions. It's a big problem for a state that, when it comes to administration, it holds a monopoly, detached from market forces. Therefore, wherever possible market forces should deliberately be brought to bear on the state, so that the laws of competition apply there, too.

4. The regulatory and the oversight functions should be separated. This is a fairly straightforward idea, meaning that the people who make the rules are not the ones responsible for overseeing their implementation. These functions should

be split between two separate institutions. This is the extension of the constitutional principle of the separation of powers to administrative relations: at no level should any even relatively unbounded power lie in the hands of one person. This is also a much more effective battle against corruption than are criminal measures.

Of course, I've listed only the most basic ideas for administrative reform, which is one of the most important tasks for any government that wants to build the new Russia. This reform cannot be put off. If there's an effectively operating state apparatus, with clearly delineated functions and strict discipline, this will create the conditions for success in all other areas. However, there is one technical problem that will hinder its creation: personnel. And, as we all know (as Stalin said), it's the personnel who decide everything.

It's impossible to build a new system of administration without the right personnel. But for various reasons the available personnel always turn out to be unsuitable. Some are clever, cunning, well trained – but unable to work in a new way and not prepared to learn new methods. Others are so set in their old ways that no talents they may have can possibly compensate for their faulty mentality. There's always been a shortage of personnel in Russia. It was always difficult to find a competent worker for any position, especially for the civil service. And as for finding a competent worker who's prepared to operate within the framework of a system that doesn't even exist yet – it's virtually impossible.

There's yet another bottleneck: new administrative technology. If we don't introduce this, we'll never change the system. For now, the whole system of administration remains totally archaic. An official's work involves carrying out registrations, deciding whether or not to issue permits, and also allocating everything that needs to be allocated. Any thinking person could fulfil these tasks if they turned their hand to it. In principle, they could all be done by a scribe from a government office in the Muscovy of old. They'd just need some computer training. Given that state functions haven't changed fundamentally since that time, it's unlikely that they'd have any problem. But if we were to carry out the administrative reforms I outlined above, then the functions of the state apparatus would change radically. For this we need a particular type of professional that simply doesn't exist in Russia – and never has.

First and foremost, we're talking here about people who can establish working interaction between state regulatory authorities, state oversight bodies and the commercial sector, who will take upon themselves the implementation of a significant amount of the state's tasks. This is how the modern world works. I have in mind here especially various public–private partnerships. It's impossible to imagine a modern state that doesn't have these now. But without highly qualified specialists who already have significant experience of this, it's impossible to set this up in Russia.

Where are we going to find these highly qualified specialists for the civil service? This is a dilemma that we've come across before. We could employ our own people, such as they are, and try to train them on the job. Or, if we could overcome our phobia, we could open the way to the civil service for foreigners who already have this experience of best-practice. If we take a sober look at Russian history we will see that all the key, decisive reforms have been solved this way. The pride and joy of the present regime, the Russian army, was created by foreign specialists at the time of Peter the Great. They were also the ones in the age of industrialization who created all the industries that today provide the army with its weaponry. At crucial moments, the Russian government didn't hold back from taking foreigners into its service when this was needed. And more often than not this approach justified itself.

The conclusion is simple: we have to follow both paths. We have to train our own people where we can and as thoroughly as we can; but while they're training, we mustn't be too afraid or embarrassed to hire foreigners. If we wish quickly to change the quality of the civil service in Russia, we have to open the door to foreign specialists. Of course, we must put in place sensible safeguards, but I can see no other solution today, especially in those areas where there's virtually no home-grown experience. In any case, we're not talking about huge numbers of people. I believe that we would need between 3,000 and 5,000 specialists in the central government, and half that number in the regions. But we mustn't repeat the mistakes made under Gorbachev and Yeltsin. We have to invite, genuinely, the best professional managers and not 'the boys from Chicago'. We have to hire the most progressive managers from international corporations and government structures all over the world, those who have practical, not just theoretical, experience of management. We must give them the chance to work for us and teach those who'll be working alongside them. I would imagine that this will take about five years, ten at the most.

If we want quality, we have to be prepared to pay for it – both our own people and the foreigners. We must offer sufficiently high salaries, so that we can demand what we want from them, including total honesty. We'll have to pay the foreigners more. But Russia is a sufficiently wealthy country that we can afford to employ in our service for a time not simply the best from among 140 million, but the best from a few billion, selecting them on an individual basis. This, incidentally, takes great skill, and we shall also have to seek the assistance of true professionals to conduct the search. I have my own experience, which I'm prepared to share. When I had to turn YUKOS into a cutting-edge international company employing best practice, the foreigners whom I invited to join us were paid more than I was. Then, of course, I recouped the costs when it came to paying dividends. But that was much later. At first, we had a great deal to learn. And we paid well for this knowledge. There is no alternative.

To sum up, I repeat again that a comprehensive administrative reform of the civil service is an issue that brooks no delay. It must be a priority for whatever government comes after the Putin regime. The aim of this reform (which incidentally was one that Putin himself called a priority, and was one of his first total failures) is to turn an archaic, semi-Soviet, semi-feudal state machine into a modern system of administration. In essence, Russia has to start from scratch to create a civil service independent of both politics and business. And in order to get it going, we need once again to do what we've done many times before in our history and invite into the Russian civil service foreigners who have the necessary knowledge and experience. Incidentally, this will be easier for us to do than it was for our predecessors. The Putin regime has forced tens of thousands of talented people out of the country. These people have gained invaluable experience in Western corporations and, in the right circumstances, can return to their Motherland.

10

What Is Meant by 'A Turn to the Left'? A Social Welfare State or a Socialist State?

I've had a great deal of time to think about mistakes – both the ones I've made and other peoples'. But it didn't take me long to find the greatest of them. Back in 2004, when I was contemplating how it was that we – and I personally – had ended up where we were, I wrote the first version of 'A Turn to the Left'. At that time, this title may have seemed a little odd. You may think that a man who had been able to make use of all the advantages that the market economy gave to enterprising people would have been just the person to write about a turn to the right (in the economic sense). But the fact is that long before my conflict with Putin's regime crossed over to its open and acute phase, I had understood clearly that, for Russia, with its history, its mentality and its traditions, an economically right-leaning liberal policy would lead it into a complete dead-end. I still hold to this view today, more than fifteen years after that first article saw the light of day.

However, with hindsight, much appears different from how it was then, and so this calls for a fresh appraisal of the situation. I now have a pretty good idea of what this left turn should begin with in Russia. So what's changed? First of all, a pseudo left-wing political course has emerged from the Kremlin, something that existed but was not evident before. This copies, yet mocks, a left-wing agenda. How should we describe Putin's regime? Left-wing? Or right-wing? I'm sure that the vast majority of people would say that Putin has a left-wing agenda. He is developing the state sector, he fights against independent businesses, he's created a complex and convoluted system of social benefits, and so on. But in actual fact, it's completely the other way round. Putin is actually continuing the traditions of the 1990s, and is following the course of a radically right-wing policy. That's why the need for a turn to the left has only increased in recent years.

In order to delve deeper into this question, we have to define what we mean by 'right' and by 'left'. And in today's world, that's no easy task. Everywhere, not just in Russia, we see right-wing politicians co-opting left-wing agendas. A textbook example is Trump with his eccentric rhetoric. The borders between right and left are blurred today; all definitions have been lost. In order to try to bring some clarity to this question, in my opinion, we have to concentrate on the main issue, and not get lost in the minutiae. And I believe that the main issue is social inequality. If a political course ultimately leads to the growth of social inequality, it's a right-wing programme, however much it is dressed up in left-wing rhetoric. But if it leads to a reduction in social inequality, it's left-wing.

Let's examine Putin's social and economic policies from this point of view. Putin came to power on an anti-oligarch agenda, which in words was and remains one of the cornerstones of Kremlin mythology. But in reality the political course he's followed not only hasn't narrowed the gap between the rich and the poor, it has increased social inequality to levels never witnessed before. Putin has placed a huge amount of economic and political power in the hands of a very narrow stratum, made up of the higher, largely *siloviki* law-enforcement and military bureaucracy and the criminal and semi-criminal 'asset-holders' who serve their interests. In place of the inequality that naturally arises because of a market economy, and that modern societies have more or less learnt to manage, Putinism has used the power it holds to create such inequality that an impenetrable wall has been built between the rich and the poor.

In Putin's Russia, the rich have got richer and the poor have got poorer more quickly than happened in Russia in the 1990s. But thanks to the growth in energy prices that resulted in a general rise in the standard of living, this process went unnoticed – up to a certain point. There was a lot of money around, and so the poor received some 'severance pay'. However, for every rouble in social handouts that the president talks about with great ceremony in his annual address to the nation, there's a dollar that goes into the pockets of Putin's elite. As a result, the distance between the richest and the poorest strata of Russian society has been steadily increasing. This process no longer goes unnoticed, because the regime has run out of money for the social sector. In recent years in Russia we've seen the growth not only of relative poverty, but also of absolute poverty. So from this point of view, over the course of twenty years, Putin has been consistently carrying out a radically right-wing policy, which can be seen objectively by the increasing stratification of society. I believe that this will lead to a dead-end and that it represents a threat to national security, since, ultimately, this, faster than any imaginary 'foreign agents', will introduce social conflict to the country.

As well as the increasing rift between the incomes of the rich and the poor, which is already in danger of causing an explosion, the whole system of distributing wealth in society is becoming warped. Raiding businesses is the very essence of the system that Putin has created, and is one of the basic sources of inequality. The government's direct involvement in this process gives rise to a latent (but no less widespread) redistribution of wealth in favour of those who demonstrate loyalty to the regime. This accelerates the degeneration not

only of economic institutions, but also of the moral foundations of society. Any immoral behaviour in this system, be it
lying, betrayal, denunciations and so on, is encouraged and
financially advantageous.

The main thing that should be understood about social
inequality in the Putin era is that, to a significant extent, at
its foundation lie non-economic factors. To a large degree,
it is artificially created inequality supported by political violence. Consequently, the only way to fight this inequality
is to eliminate the political factors that give rise to it. So all
the propaganda efforts that the Kremlin puts into this battle
against poverty can be seen as nothing short of a charade. The
main precondition for an effective battle against poverty in
Russia is to remove the regime that has, by its very existence,
created and increased this poverty. The regime has acted like
an enormous pump, sucking money out of the pockets of millions of its citizens and pouring it into the pockets of Putin's
millionaires.

How has this pump been constructed? From where exactly
is it hoovering up resources? The answer is pretty obvious: the
regime sustains and enriches itself mainly from its exploitation of resource rent without any oversight. It divides up the
profits from the sale of raw materials – oil, gas, metals and
timber – in a completely arbitrary fashion, doing simply as it
wishes and acting in the interests of a narrow circle of people.
I believe that, in order for Russia to be a state that provides for
its people – as is prescribed in the Constitution, but doesn't
exist in reality – it's vital that society be given back control
over resource rent – that is, over the rent proceeds from the
extraction and exploitation of the country's natural resources.

The idea of giving control over resource rent back to society isn't new. The Communists write and talk about this a
great deal. The question is, do we genuinely give this control
to society, or do we return it once again to the state? If we
return it to the state, then once again control will be in the

hands of another small group of people – just a different group this time. And even though the Communists' idea that everything should once again be nationalized seems a fairer solution than what we have today, it would lead to another historical dead-end for Russia. A return to the USSR would inevitably lead once again to a bureaucratized, sluggish and inefficient economy, which is what destroyed the Soviet Union. This is inevitable with any gigantic state monopoly, especially in a country where the corporate culture is so undeveloped, where the government bureaucracy is poorly educated and economically illiterate, and where, what's more, there's a centuries-old tradition of corruption and sabotage.

But this is not the only issue. The principal drawback to what the Communists are proposing – that is, marching into the future by way of the past – is a bureaucratic equation that cannot be solved politically: the more resources that are concentrated in the hands of the state, the greater is the state's role in their redistribution. And the greater the state's role in their redistribution, then the greater the quantity of resource rent society never sees because it's needed to fund this huge redistribution system. This means that, from the point of view both of society itself and of each individual citizen, this whole reverse nationalization makes no sense at all. The lion's share of resource rent will continue to be spent to provide for the state's huge power structure; another part of it will be wasted because of the inefficiency of the state monopoly; and the crumbs that are left will go to the people in return for their giving up their rights as citizens. The question as to who will be the face of this machine for theft and deception – whether it would be Putin's followers or Zyuganov's followers or someone else – has little significance for Russia's fate.

How can we break this vicious circle and tear the rents from Russia's natural wealth out of the hands of the criminal bureaucrats? I believe there is a solution, and it's a fairly obvious one. It's not much use either to those who are currently in power, or to those who hope to take over in the future. The people who would benefit are those in today's Russia who are deprived of proper political representation, and whose voice, therefore, is never heard. I think that the only possible solution to the problem of what to do with resource rents in Russia is to lock them into the social needs of the population. This would cut out the state's role as the middle-man in their redistribution.

And such a possibility genuinely exists in Russia.

If we roughly compare the proceeds that Putin's regime receives today from resource rents with the amount that the government should be paying for pensions but cannot cover, then the sums are virtually the same. On the expenditure side we can also add in spending on medical insurance, which the government also isn't able to meet, and which it is therefore constantly cutting back. Given this, wouldn't it be simpler to cut out all the intermediate stages and direct the windfall prof-its from resource rents – in the main, those from raw materials, notably oil and gas – straight to people's pension and health savings accounts? Then, when the need arises, either when they reach pensionable age or are ill, people would receive the necessary funds. What's more, this would be proper sums of money, not simply the crumbs that prevent them from dying of starvation.

Technically, this wouldn't be difficult to arrange. Already today, the windfall profits from the sale of raw materials are earmarked separately, and come into the state coffers in a separate line from the companies that receive resource rent, so it wouldn't be difficult to keep them separate (it would simply be about the inefficiency of Putin's managers). Today they are merged into the overall budget flow, and the government dis-poses of them as it wishes, spending them on crazy Kremlin projects or just simply stealing them. But they should instead be distributed equally on a monthly basis into the savings accounts of every citizen of the country.

These savings accounts, pension and health, should be opened the moment a person is born and last until they die. This would be a genuine privilege of Russian citizenship, rather than an imaginary symbol of belonging to a great country. We have to create a situation where being a citizen of Russia would mean having the privilege of living with dignity into old age, and not just of dying to protect 'the Rotenbergs' palaces' in a series of endless and pointless wars entered into by the regime. Today, resource rent drops into a black hole, where it's redistributed in the most outrageous fashion to the beneficiaries of Putin's regime. We must make this black hole transparent, so that every citizen can see and understand what's happening with the national heritage that's been handed down by our ancestors.

The sums of money that would be saved in these accounts would be very significant. All around the world pension funds are important investment vehicles, and I don't see why Russia should be an exception. I suggest that idle cash could be held temporarily in a Russian index fund (a consolidated packet of Russian securities, traded on the stock market), which would in turn support Russian production. In this way a safety cushion would be created that would genuinely help to turn Russia away from being a socialist state, where the country's wealth of raw materials belong to the bureaucrats, into a proper social welfare state, where resource rent belongs to the people, and comes under the direct control of society.

I'd like to repeat what exactly I see as the difference between the model of a socialist state – with no prospects for the future – and a social welfare state, which not only concerns what's written in the Constitution, but is in actual fact the only suitable way for the economic system in Russia today to develop.

In a socialist state, production and distribution are in the hands of an inefficient monopoly that does everything in the interests of a bureaucratic clan. In a social welfare state, on the other hand, the state takes neither production nor distribution under its control, thus encouraging competition in all areas. The state's responsibility lies simply in setting the rules in order to lessen social inequality.

On the surface, some of these suggestions reflect the slogans of the left-wing opposition to Putin's regime, including the Russian Communists. The latter also call for the re-establishment of public oversight over resource rent; but, as I mentioned earlier, they propose doing this in the same way the Bolsheviks carried out nationalization, by putting control over resources into the hands of the state. While I agree with the left insofar as it is essential to re-establish public oversight over natural resources, I cannot agree with the way in which they want to do it. As I see it, this wouldn't level out inequality, but simply turn it from one economic form into another one dominated by the *nomenklatura* and their clans.

Unlike a socialist state, a social welfare state doesn't try to make everyone equal in order then to work out who are more equal than others. The aim of a social welfare state is to give everyone an equal chance to develop and succeed. Had I written this text fifteen or twenty years ago, I would probably have ended the sentence right there. But given the experience that I've gained today, I'll expand on this. Equal opportunities to succeed should be given to all those who are ready to use them. But those who cannot do this, or just don't want to, should be given minimal guarantees. Without this humanitarian component, no modern social welfare state can exist, especially in Russia.

To summarize briefly, let me explain why I believe we need to make a left turn at the current stage of development of Russian statehood. We need it in order to remove the political factors that are leading to an explosive growth in social inequality, and we need to start following a consistent path aimed at reducing this inequality. Naturally, I consider the most important thing we need to do is to get rid of Putin's system, including its 'corporate raids' with the use of the law-enforcement agencies, which allows for the redistribution by non-economic means of national wealth among groups of people who are loyal to the regime, leading to it being concentrated in the hands of a small clique that controls the state.

Immediately after this first condition has been carried out, the interim government should resolve the question of how to restore public oversight over resource rent. As I wrote above, I see the most sensible and efficient way of doing this as being the creation of lifelong insurance savings accounts for everyone, into which the windfall profits from raw materials can be paid directly in equal amounts. Deciding this issue will be just as important as dealing with the question of property ownership, which took place during the social revolution in Russia at the start of the twentieth century. But this time it must really be solved in the interests of the whole nation, and not just those in the vanguard. This is the only thing that will give the interim government the genuine support of the people as a whole, and create that political 'safety cushion' that will allow it to carry out all the other long overdue economic and political reforms.

11

How to Achieve Economic Justice: Nationalization or Honest Privatization?

Total restoration of social justice is impossible without an accompanying restoration of economic justice. In the widest sense of the term, economic justice is the most important part of social justice. And in the narrower sense, it signifies equality, not so much in the distribution of national wealth, as in having access to the basic means of its production. In other words, it's economic justice that gives people a more even chance of becoming rich.

The logic here is simple: those who hold the basic tools needed for the production of wealth inevitably have a massive advantage when it comes to their distribution. And this can't be balanced out by any subsequent corrective measures such as taxes or subsidies or the like.

Therefore, the question of property – who should hold the basic means of production of national wealth, and on what basis? – always had, still has, and always will have the greatest significance for society. Whatever government takes over from Putin's regime simply cannot ignore this.

There's no need to explain that the privatization process that began in Russia in the 1990s, and that in reality is still going on, led to the destruction of economic justice. In an instant, it created a deep inequality for different strata of society in terms of access to the basic means of production. It proved very difficult to get rid of this. This is not only an objective factor that any future government has to face up to (the current one should as well), but it's also a challenge that it must tackle.

I should add from my own observations that, for various post-Soviet generations, privatization was, and clearly remains, a serious psychological trauma that has left a deep scar on society's consciousness. So, in any crisis, the question of who owns the bulk of Russia's national wealth, and why it's in the hands of these people, will always rise to the surface. And it will always be impossible to avoid answering this question – as so it should be.

Looking back with the advantage of hindsight at what happened more than a quarter of a century ago, I consider that the privatization of the Soviet economy – or, to be more accurate, the removal of state ownership – was an inevitable and justifiable action. But I suggest that the way in which it was carried out was unacceptable for society, unfair economically, and harmful to the economic and historical development of the country.

The post-Soviet privatization de facto presented advantages in access to assets to a very narrow circle of people. For a variety of reasons, these people found themselves in a winning position: administrative resources were available to them; they had access to funds; they were well educated; they were still young; and so on. On the other hand, the broad mass of the people had no possibility of taking part in the distribution of these assets right from the start. They were reduced to being temporary holders of vouchers, that they either sold off to speculators at a low cost that didn't reflect their genuine economic value, or they lost out altogether and their grandchildren were left with these worthless pieces of paper as a memento of the era. Individual shares in investment funds were simply a myth that was shattered by the economic crisis of 1998.

The far more successful privatizations that took place in Eastern Europe demonstrate that there was an alternative to the method chosen in Russia. But the decision taken in Russia was less a mistake than it was a conscious ideological choice. The government made solving a political issue its number one priority, not solving a social or an economic problem. The aim was to pull the rug out from under the feet of the Communists, whose main support came from the so-called 'red directors' of large Soviet-era state enterprises, by rapidly creating a new class of owners.

I think we can say that the Russian government of the time deliberately chose this method of privatization because it was the one that best met its priorities. At that time, it hardly bothered anyone that, as a result of this, economic justice was thrown out of the window and, along with it, social justice. Similarly, no one cared that this created the conditions for the rise of a crime-ridden economy and a mafia state. All these fruits ripened about fifteen years later, notably after Putin came to power.

Long before Putin, the authorities skilfully conducted the privatization process, using it as an instrument to strengthen their influence over society. And, a priori, the privatization of strategically important enterprises was a subject for political bargaining, something the government used to solve its own issues, which were frequently far removed from economic ones. Loans-for-shares auctions, which became a bargaining chip in the 1996 presidential election campaign, were no exception.

As someone who was directly engaged in this game with the government as a representative of business, I had understood by the beginning of this century that the country had entered a social and political dead-end. It was vital to get out of this by putting right the results of this slapdash privatization. I began to speak out, saying that it was essential to take urgent and extraordinary steps in order to re-establish economic justice.

Soon after Putin came to power, I suggested to the leadership of the country that we should look again at the issue of privatization; in the first instance, of course, that of the loans-for-shares auctions. I suggested that the problem could be solved by bringing in a one-off tax for the main beneficiaries of the privatization process. This could be done by way of contributions to a special fund for economic development, that would have been measured in tens of billions of dollars.

Unfortunately, not only was my initiative not supported, but it became one of the factors that led to my arrest. Later, I and others realized that Putin's regime had no intention of changing the results of privatization; on the contrary, they planned to use them specifically for their own ends. This strengthened my sense of foreboding, and ultimately led me to the conclusions that I laid out in my article 'A Turn to the Left', which I wrote when I was in prison.

In the more than fifteen years that have passed since the publication of 'A Turn to the Left', the situation in Russia has radically changed; what began as a political error has ended up being a full-blown political and socioeconomic disaster. Clearly, the measures that I suggested at the start of the century are totally inadequate today. Tough and serious decisions need to be taken, and political will and courage are needed to make them happen.

Twenty years of Putin in power show that the main beneficiary of the privatization process that was launched at the start of the 1990s has been Putin himself. Once he came to power, he and a narrow group of people close to him – some of whom were directly linked to the criminal underworld – privatized not individual enterprises, or even the economy: they privatized the state itself. They turned the state into a tool for their own personal enrichment and for their own common use.

Today 'the state', in the strict meaning of the word, has ceased to exist in Russia. It's become an enormous private militarized corporation, solving the problems of its principal shareholders. The whole world now knows about Yevgeny Prigozhin's private military company known as the Wagner Group, and that it represents a miniature version of the whole of the Putin state. The state in Russia doesn't defend the national interests, but simply serves the interests of the clan that runs it.

From the first days of its existence, this corporation in the guise of a state busied itself with what it regarded as the most important task: the redistribution of property to its main shareholders. This process, which has been going on for more than twenty years, has brought us to the point where Russia's fundamental national wealth is now under the control of a very small group of people, probably just a few hundred families. These people represent the backbone of Putin's infamous 'power vertical'.

In a matter of years, Russia became the country with the highest concentration of capital. But this capital was tied in with power; if someone lost their access to power, then they inevitably lost their economic influence too. So every business group that was close to the centre of power in Russia became vertically integrated into the whole power structure, especially into the block of law-enforcement and military ministries. It worked the other way round too. Every area of bureaucracy built up underneath itself its own business infrastructure. For Putin's regime, money became simply a function of power.

At the same time, we can speak with confidence about the collective ownership by the ruling clan over the property it controls. Russia's economy today is run along the principle of a thieves' 'collective fund'. It doesn't matter who's registered as the official owner; what matters is who it is 'understood' to belong to. A perfect illustration of this is the story of the ill-fated palace in Gelendzhik. It was felt necessary to pass ownership from one member of Putin's circle to another; but everyone knows that it doesn't belong to either of them.

Putin and his team conducted a further, secret, privatization in Russia, by carrying out a secondary seizure of assets to their benefit. They achieved this in two ways. First of all, Putin re-recruited the vast majority of the old 'boyars' – the leaders of the former elite. These were the main shareholders of the financial and industrial groups that emerged in the 1990s. Putin turned them into nothing more than mere asset-holders, dependent on his authority. Either they would carry out his orders, or they would lose their property. Next, Putin created a new nobility from among his 'servants' – people such as Igor Sechin, Alexey Miller, the Rotenbergs and the Kovalchuks. They were given direct control over part of the state's assets, as well as over the assets seized from obstinate boyars.

In time, the difference between the boyars and the nobility more or less disappeared, and now has a merely decorative meaning. Nowadays, nearly everyone with a large fortune in Russia is fully and directly beholden to the ruling political clan, is an integral part of it, and de facto merely the holder of property that actually belongs to the clan as a whole.

This mafia-type property structure is completely incompatible with any pretence at building any kind of normal state system in Russia at the basis of which would lie the principle of justice. It prevents the construction of any such system, and would destroy the efforts of any government, even if these efforts were utterly sincere.

The longer this goes on, the more this parasitic system of collective ownership of property by the ruling clan is turning into an unbearable weight on society. This tumour that's preventing the country's development has to be removed, in the interests of Russian society and in the interests of Russia's future. Many people understand this now. It's discussed in kitchens and in the smoking rooms of universities. It's the obvious political imperative of our time, even if for now it's hidden from view.

As soon as society wakes up, the first thing the people will demand of any interim government is that it do away with ownership of property by this criminal gang that's running the Russian state. And whether it wants to or not, the government will be obliged to do this. But how can this be accomplished without repeating the mistakes of those who carried out the privatizations of the 'nineties? After all, maybe they too had wanted things to turn out better than they did

The most widely discussed and perhaps seemingly most obvious way to proceed is through nationalization. This might well appear to be the easiest solution: take it all back and hand it over to the state. But where will that lead us as a result? We'll just go back to where we were: the USSR in the middle of the last century (and that's the best-case scenario). Once again, we'll have a huge, unwieldy economy, run by a sluggish bunch of bureaucrats who'll try to squeeze as many privileges out of the system as they can.

After nationalization, these bureaucrats will once again become *nomenklatura* oligarchs, even if, strictly speaking, they don't own the property that they're controlling. This can end only one way: in exactly the same sort of crisis that finished off the Soviet Union.

There are better solutions that simply haven't been tried. Russia doesn't need nationalization, but a new, honest and fair, form of privatization. The interim government's task lies in creating a platform for such a privatization to take place.

Under the new regime, all the property currently held by this criminal gang that calls itself the authorities in Russia must be expropriated. I can see no alternative to this harsh measure. The basis and scope of this expropriation will have to be carefully worked out in the future, but they will be extensive. All this property should be placed temporarily in a fund under public control.

All escheated property must also be placed there – enterprises that are controlled by clans dependent on the state that in reality have been bankrupt for a long time, but have been kept afloat only by direct and indirect subsidies from the state budget. By my reckoning, today both categories together account for up to half of the total national wealth – a significant sum.

The most difficult task, though, is not the seizure of these assets, but how to deal with them efficiently. I suggest that none of this confiscated property should be handed directly to the state, where it will be managed by bureaucrats; instead, it should be put into independent unit investment funds under direct public control. It is likely that several such funds will be needed, around ten or so. Some of them could be organized on the basis of certain industries. The principal criterion should be economic expediency. Every citizen of the country who reaches adulthood would become a unit holder in these funds.

Creating nationwide unit investment funds from these confiscated assets is an emergency and temporary measure. It's a one-off action to re-establish economic justice. Therefore, it's the generation alive today who should benefit most from this. Every citizen should receive their units of each of these funds, along the lines of the voucher system. But they won't be allowed to cash in their units immediately. A moratorium will have to be enforced to prevent divestiture and to stabilize both the situation and, consequently, the value of the units. It is vital not to allow a repeat of what happened thirty years ago.

After a certain period of time, the moratorium will be lifted and people will have the opportunity to sell off their units, receiving equal and fair compensation. Those who don't live long enough to see this day should have the right to pass on their units as inheritance. This will maintain for them, too, the principle of justice. Selling units during the moratorium period should be allowed only in exceptional circumstances and under conditions provided for by a special law (for example, a *force majeure*).

Before the moratorium is lifted, these funds should work as normal commercial enterprises, the aim of which is to make a profit. Profits received should be reinvested in the fund. But part of the profits may be used as extra social insurance for the unit holders. Which events would be covered by insurance and the amount that should be paid if they occur would be established by law each year, depending also on the financial condition of the funds. It is most likely that this would cover expenses such as long-term medical treatment, for which, today, the state and society collect money according to the principle of 'every little bit helps' – although somehow funds are always found for palaces and missiles.

The management structure of the funds should be on two levels. Each fund should have a supervisory board, whose members would be appointed directly by parliament. The responsibilities of the supervisory board would be limited. They would appoint a management company and take decisions on the acquisition or disposal of core assets. At some stage, the sale of assets would become a valuable source of income for the funds, but this could happen only once normal economic conditions are in place.

All the day-to-day management of the funds would be concentrated in the hands of the management companies, which would have been selected following a tender, carried out in line with a special law. The management companies would have just one goal: efficient management and maximization of profits, from where the unit holders would be paid dividends. When necessary, they should also prepare the property owned by the funds for a future privatization – a normal, economically based, transparent privatization, approved by society.

It would be unwise and inadvisable for the expropriated assets to be sold off too soon, since the sale of property during the crisis conditions of the transition period would inevitably happen only at incommensurately low prices. We all witnessed this in the 1990s. Therefore, the property owned by the unit funds should be frozen, and exiting the funds with compensation would be allowed only in exceptional cases and in extreme circumstances. Later on, and not before five or ten years have passed, a new, honest, privatization of these assets should take place, one that could be acknowledged as a sound decision. This would finally bring an end to the long-drawn-out argument about the fate of the privatization of the 'nineties.

The task of the interim government would be to give back to society direct control over the national wealth, and to destroy the parasitical ownership by criminal gangs. If it's unable to cope with this task, then it's unlikely to win the trust of society for everything else.

Part II

How Do We Avoid Creating a New Dragon?

If you think about it, the dragon isn't actually a malicious creature, but a symbol for the state. It's the type of state where its three heads – the legislative, the executive and the judicial – are firmly attached to the one fat, corrupt body of the mighty bureaucratic machine. And thanks to the unity of its heads, it can walk all over a fragmented society. In order to establish society's control over the state, it's essential, on the one hand, to unite people around the idea of citizenship (in other words, to turn the crowd into a civil society), and, on the other, to tear all three of these heads of governmental authority from the bureaucratic body and force them to live separately. This is no easy task. Because, over the many centuries of Russian autocracy, these three heads have become such a part of this absolutist body that neither they themselves nor anyone around them can imagine how they can be made independent of each other. One reason why there has to be a transitional period, therefore, is to learn how to do this. And if we don't do this, then it won't be a transitional period, but simply an operation to transplant the dragon's heads. The dragon will survive, and, after a short period of rehabilitation, will once again return to doing what it always does. In order to prevent this from happening, society must take upon itself the responsibility for the choice it will make when solving the most difficult problems that Russian history has set it.

How Do We Avoid
Creating a New Dragon?

12

The Choice of Civilization:
An Empire or a Nation-State?

For the past 500 years, from the time of Tsar Ivan the Terrible, Russia has been an empire; that is, a country made up of various parts that differ from each other in culture and in their sociopolitical make-up, and are kept together not so much by a desire to live together but simply by armed force.

All the generations alive today as well as the dozens of generations that came before them have known nothing but empire, and couldn't even imagine any other type of political system. And whenever the empire suddenly became weak, it generally led to turmoil, destruction and civil war, which all brought greater troubles than all the problems of the empire taken together.

On every occasion, the turmoil ended with the creation of new, more ambitious and more aggressive empires. The Romanov Empire took the place of the Rurikid Tsardom of Muscovy; the Romanovs, in their turn, were replaced by the Bolsheviks. Between each of these periods there was a terrifying civil war. People in Russia have grown used to living in an empire. They trust it, and they see it as saving society from destruction and disorder.

What's more, they don't believe in themselves. They don't believe that they can live without a 'tsar' (it doesn't matter whether he's called the Emperor, the General Secretary, or the President), with his iron fist, his police, his army and his bureaucracy. They don't believe the promises of those who call for freedom and democracy, because on a deep level they remember that the alternative to empire is turmoil, destruction and chaos.

But while Russia was building and destroying empires, building even more powerful empires and destroying them again, the world around it was radically changing. As a way of governing, empires were disappearing. In their place came the concept of the nation-state – that is, countries where a single culture dominates (the language, the literature and everyday practices), and people wish to live according to one set of laws and on one territory (I'll say more later about some of the ideas that have arisen, such as multiculturalism, not entirely successfully, in recent years).

Suddenly Russia was just about the only empire still left on the planet; a kind of medieval 'Last of the Mohicans'.

Today, Russia is surrounded by peoples whose lives are arranged according to completely different principles from those of empire – and not only do they not perish, they flourish. Although these nation-states have plenty of their own problems, the gap between them and 'the last empire' is growing at a headlong pace, in terms of economic and technological progress, in their levels of education and health care, and more basically in their citizens' longevity and quality of life. With each day that passes, the chasm grows wider, and the day is not far off when the gap will become disastrous, unbridgeable for one or even two generations.

In the near future, those who have been born and live on what has become 'the edge of Russian civilization', and who are responsible for the country's future, are facing an epoch-changing choice between living in an empire and living in a nation-state. They will have to answer the following question: do they wish to maintain traditions, and therefore try at any cost to rebuild their crumbling empire? Or are they prepared to ditch their traditions, kick the empire onto the rubbish heap of history, and attempt to build their own nation-state in its place?

This truly is akin to Hamlet's question. The choice is between the old world, which may be imperfect and condemned to death, but one with which people are familiar in every last detail; and a seductive, unknown world, which promises much, yet at the same time is frightening. The problem for the current generations in Russia is not that they don't like the actual choice (which is only natural; no one likes having to choose between death or change), but that they don't have the opportunity to put it off and pass the responsibility for the fate of our Russian civilization onto the shoulders of their children and grandchildren.

Russia is at the crossroads of civilizations. The choice between an empire and a nation-state is a fundamental choice of civilization. It opens the way for answers to dozens of other questions. These may be less global in scope, but they are the complicated issues that are facing Russian society in the early years of the twenty-first century. If this choice is not made now – or if the wrong choice is made – then there will be no choice for their children and grandchildren to make.

My choice for Russia is that of the nation-state; a choice for the future, not the past.

The Russia of my dreams is an association of people of different ethnic backgrounds who are brought together by an internal civilizational unity, for whom what they have in common is more important than their differences; it is not an empire, kept together by a steel ring of militarized bureaucracy, like an old cracked barrel. I don't deny that the Russia of our children could still exist in the creaking shell of an empire. But if we want our grandchildren to see Russia, then we need to create something else: a state based on a genuine (and not an imaginary) desire for people to live together inside a space where there are shared values of language, culture, law and politics.

I reject nostalgia for the empire, be it open or dressed up in pseudo-democratic and pseudo-liberal garb. The creation of a Russian nation-state is the greatest historical task that Russians and the other peoples who live in the country have been insistently, but inconsistently, trying to accomplish for centuries, and one that has to be accomplished once and for all by the generations alive today. We now live under such historical constraints that this decision can no longer be put off: it's now or never. Either we do it, or no one will.

Russia needs something more than an empire where the people are kept down by forces that are outside the needs of society – the army, the police and the bureaucracy, all of which give the appearance of order on its territory.

The stronger an empire is, the more all-encompassing it is, and the more uniform its political space. But the weaker it is, the more exceptions there are to the overall rules: so there's one rule for Moscow, something else for Chechnya, a third one for Crimea, and so forth. The unity of the empire is an illusion, and it's only symbolically embodied in the figure of its supreme ruler, inevitably producing the impression of being someone sacred: 'There is Putin, therefore there is Russia', and vice versa.

In place of the symbolic unity of 'political nationhood', represented by proxy by an irremovable 'national leader', the nation should be genuinely united, not in need of a 'senior policeman-tsar' exercising absolute control over his subjects. The unity of a political (civil) nation doesn't come from outside but from within, and not with the help of an army of officials, police and soldiers, but through direct political links that arise in a society that's free of dictatorship.

The unity of a political nation, as opposed to the unity of 'political nationhood' is elementary: it is not created by the state; rather, the nation creates the state, it constitutes it. That is why a state created by the nation, as opposed to a state that controls the nation, becomes a genuine constitutional entity. For such a state to emerge, a consensus is needed – the agreement of the majority on the fundamental values and principles of the social structure. The person who agrees to accept the basic principles of the Constitution as their own, and who's prepared to defend them if necessary even by taking up arms, becomes a citizen; and a people that is made up of such citizens becomes a nation.

The peoples of Russia are in the process of creating a Russian nation – but they haven't got there yet. The USSR endeavoured to create something new in history: the Soviet people. However, since this project was part of the totalitarian Communist project that rejected the fundamental Constitutional norms necessary for creating a nation, it failed. People simply refused to consider the principles of Communist totalitarianism as their own.

Today, we have to solve this issue again, but within the framework of a Constitution, and not through terror.

A nation-state can emerge only as a result of the free self-determination of all the peoples of Russia. Citizens must be given a genuine possibility to make a conscious decision, based on all the information available –not false information, as happened in 1993, nor the insulting views put forward later. They have to decide whether they are ready to live in a united state according to the principles laid down by a common Constitution, or whether they want to continue to make their own history, with all of the benefits and hardships this brings. This is a serious test and brings great political stress, but there's no way round it. You can't build castles on sand.

So in order to create a nation-state in Russia, three historically important steps must be taken:

1. The concept of empire must be rejected and conditions for a free choice for the peoples of Russia must be created.

2. A genuine act for the establishment of the new Russia must be passed. This was what the Constituent Assembly was prevented from doing one hundred years ago because it was dissolved by the Bolsheviks. Perhaps a new Constituent Assembly will have to be created for this, activating a 'dormant norm' of the current Constitution.

3. Radical constitutional and judicial reforms need to be carried out, so as to create the political and legal infrastructure of the Russian nation-state.

The nation-state is the state of all the peoples of Russia who declare that it is their desire and their will to become its co-founders. It will have nothing in common with a state that is founded on privilege based on blood or belief. However, it cannot ignore the simple fact that the political space out of which it has grown was formed by the active participation of the ethnic Russian nationality and is based on that culture.

Being too embarrassed to acknowledge this historical fact is as mistaken and unacceptable as would be trying to drag some kind of political advantage out of it and creating unlawful privileges for the 'titular nationality'.

For almost half a century Europe has tried to solve such questions under the banner of multiculturalism. This played an important role in the struggle against xenophobia and the general relaxation of morals. But as events have shown in recent years, notably the crisis over immigration, multiculturalism isn't a panacea. This is because, too frequently, it ignores the obvious fact that modern societies don't develop in a cultural vacuum, but within certain cultural traditions that have developed throughout history. These traditions, which are the basis for all the other elements of culture, deserve to be treated with respect. Therefore, it's important for Russia to include in the philosophy of multiculturalism the principle of cultural integration, to provide for harmonious relations between different ethnic groups and beliefs, on the basis of their being flexibly included into the general space of Russian culture.

The ability to speak the Russian language freely and a knowledge of the basic facts of Russian history and culture, as well as an awareness of basic economic, political and legal knowledge, and a willingness to accept the fundamental legal norms and traditions of Russian society: these should all be mandatory requirements for obtaining Russian citizenship.

These demands in no way undermine the dignity and interests of the other peoples of Russia, each of whom will be granted guarantees and conditions for the unhindered development of the language and ethnic culture of their forebears, as well as their own self-governance at the local level.

One of the most important functions of school – and, indeed, the whole system of education – is to teach people how to be citizens. And I mean 'citizens', not simply the obedient subjects of yet another autocrat. The nation-state is as far away from the empire, with its devotion to a supreme ruler who secures his place by stick and carrot, as it is from the Cossack communities of freemen, the so-called 'failed state', where everyone set their own rules. The first task of the nation state is to guarantee order and the safety of the individual at a higher level than is the case in the empire, where, behind the façade of legality, lies arbitrary lawlessness, often motivated by corruption.

In a genuine nation-state, citizens are proud to identify themselves first and foremost with their country, and only after that with their ethnicity, tribe or clan, home territory or profession.

I spent a month in a prison cell with Colonel Vladimir Kvachkov, a military intelligence officer and veteran of the war in Afghanistan, who became known throughout the country after being accused of the attempted assassination of Anatoly Chubais, and even of organizing a military coup.

We're people from different worlds and with different opinions; you could say we are fierce opponents (to put it mildly).

But when we discussed the question as to why our authorities and our society are so afraid of our own special forces – *spetsnaz* – while the Americans aren't afraid of theirs, he summed it up in a way that I still remember fifteen years later:

> The American special forces soldier sees himself first and foremost as a citizen of the USA, and only then as a member of the special forces. This is natural. If something happens to him, then he'll be protected as an American citizen. The Russian, though, is convinced that the opposite will happen. If something happens to you, don't expect any help from the state. The best you can hope for is that your friends and fellow soldiers will come to your aid. So our officers are special forces soldiers first, and citizens only after that, while for the Americans it's the other way round.

The Russia of my dreams will be re-established by citizens who want to organize their lives together. People for whom the national interest is more important than that of their social class, their corporation or their tribe. People who understand that it's better to be together than to be apart.

13

The Geopolitical Choice:
To Be a Superpower or to Consider
the National Interests?

If you travel beyond the Moscow Ring Road, you quickly find yourself in a different country. If Moscow can rival any modern European capital in terms of its urban infrastructure and public services, then outside it there lies a different Russia, a Russia inhabited by 120 million people, which looks like a picture from a film about post-war Europe – poverty-stricken and destroyed. It's difficult to believe that you're looking at a country that was the victor in the most terrifying and bloody war in the history of mankind.

How did we arrive at this? Why, thirty years after our 'victory' over Communism, after twenty years of an unchanged new 'elite' running the country, with their 'cool heads and clean hands', after years of an unbroken and completely unimaginable abundance fuelled by oil, the price of which was three times higher than the average Soviet and early Russian price: why does this other Russia lie in ruins? After all, Germany was defeated in the war, yet despite being occupied by the Americans, by 1965 West Germany had a higher standard of living than most of Europe, and its industry had pretty well returned to the position it had had previously. Why did the

Russian provinces, which hadn't been occupied by anyone, not begin to live better?

There are many reasons for this. There's the inability to manage, widespread theft, the ubiquitous monopoly – and as well as all that, there's been a serious mistake in the choice of political priorities, making the most important of them the messianic plan to re-establish Russia as a superpower.

This new idea of autocracy didn't appear out of nowhere. Determined to use any means possible to prevent the geopolitical transition of Ukraine, Russia's ruling clan opened up along the way new 'mineral deposits', ones that were much more profitable than oil or gas, under the title of 'Russia's greatness'. Since then, the authorities have been mining this seemingly inexhaustible (to them) 'fuel' in Russia in industrial amounts. It's proved to be ideal for the engine of Russia's authoritarian power.

In 2014 Russia swapped one social contract for another. To the old contract of 'stability in place of freedom', which had been the case in Russia since 2003, the Kremlin made a significant addition: 'greatness in place of justice and prosperity'. So the new social contract runs as follows: 'greatness and stability in place of freedom, justice and prosperity'. Russia's greatness now justifies all of the regime's villainy: arbitrary rule, corruption, cultural decay and backwardness. This all has to be tolerated in exchange for the ability to push Ukraine around, to shit on 'the American bastards' in Syria and Libya, and to place 'our' private armies all over Africa and even, it's rumoured, in Venezuela.

Why did Russian society agree to this deal so easily? It seems that people were ready for such a turn of events, and were even impatiently waiting for it. It's indicative that after the 'return' of Crimea in 2014, the majority of those living in Russia experienced genuine euphoria. This joy was genuine, not just imaginary. But it happened not only because people considered that annexation of Crimea restored historical justice, but also because they had grown tired of defeats, and longed for victories. It seemed to them that it was not Crimea that had been returned to them, but Russia itself – the Russia that they'd known before. This sense that strength had been restored was more important for many than the joy at the capture of Crimea, something that, up until that point, hardly anyone had thought about. If they had, it was simply as a place to go for their holidays, although in any case if they had the opportunity many preferred to go to Egypt or Turkey.

There's nothing surprising in this reaction. For centuries, Russia had been an empire, and its subjects were brought up in the tradition of empire. To this day, the majority of people find it hard to imagine that there could be any alternative to the imperial way of thinking. This is not only a Russian problem. Other former empires have encountered similar challenges, and continue to do so. (A clear illustration of this are the events in Britain in recent years around Brexit.) But in today's Russia, which had not long before experienced the collapse of the USSR, these processes proved even more destructive than anywhere else.

The birth of the new post-Soviet world was painful and accompanied by great difficulties, both for society and for the state itself. The inevitable challenges that a transition period brings were compounded by the negative effects of the huge number of strategic and tactical errors made by the leaders of the new Russia. As a result, the economy drastically imploded and the institutions of state failed, which in turn led to all aspects of life – society's and the state's – falling into criminal hands. At that time, the country not only lost a sizeable part of its territory, but also, for a long time, stopped playing any significant role in world affairs. It was as if it went from being centre stage to backstage.

The central government's defeat in the military campaign in Chechnya and the fiasco of Russia's foreign policy in the Balkans were two very powerful stimuli evoking imperial nostalgia. People regarded each of these events as a national humiliation. This led to the emergence of a sort of 'Versailles syndrome' in society – the sense that was felt in Germany after the defeat in the First World War. Instead of seeing itself as a country that could be justifiably proud of achieving a major revolution that had overthrown Communism throughout Europe, Russia mistakenly saw itself as the country that had lost the Cold War.

There were two possible ways for Russia to emerge from this post-imperial crisis, which in itself wasn't unique. It could either spend all its resources on a parody, creating the illusion of strength and an apparent rebirth, while simply pushing into the background the ruins of the old society; or it could go through a deep spiritual, socioeconomic and political transformation and genuinely become strong.

The Germans tried both paths. They went down the first one after the First World War, and it led to a national disaster. They tried the other one after the Second World War, and it led to the rebirth of the nation. The first path was directly linked to the past. It was the path of revanchism and militarism, the forcible reawakening of worn-out historical processes. The second was linked to the future. It was a way of reassessing matters and searching for new solutions.

Unfortunately, in Russia it was not the constructive, but the reconstructive scenario that was played out. At the start of the twenty-first century the ruling clan tied society to the first path, the revanchist one, and started to promote the elixir of 'greatness'. The superpower drug worked. For some years, society wandered around in a state of endless psychosis, revelling in its imaginary superiority over other peoples and a sense of might that didn't actually exist (especially after seeing Putin's famous cartoons about the power of Russian weapons). However, tiredness soon sank in, along with an awareness that Russia was having to pay an exorbitant price for these illusions, and will continue to do so in the future.

The Kremlin doesn't want to achieve Russia's greatness by developing its manufacturing potential, or by encouraging its education and science to flourish, or by revitalizing its culture. All it wants to do to make Russia great again is to employ brutal military might and nuclear blackmail. It shows its level of sophistication and inventiveness by waging a 'Scythian war' without rules, what's become known as 'hybrid war'. To do this, it mercilessly uses the military-technical potential that it inherited from the USSR, that might last another twenty or thirty years – in other words, to the end of the lives of today's Russian rulers. They couldn't care less about what comes after them. But this should be of concern to society and that part of the elite who are capable of looking beyond the horizon of their own greed and vanity.

Criticism of this new post-Soviet militarism comes either from a generally humanistic position – pacifism – or from the thought that these Kremlin ambitions are impractical – utopian – and that Russia can't wage war on the whole of humanity and will simply end up killing itself, as the USSR did. This is both true (in the long-term view) and untrue (in the short- to mid-term view). Generally, Russia's military adventures are not costing it a great deal. I can show with figures that, for now, these military provocations (with the exception of Ukraine) were not particularly burdensome for Russia. For example, its 'investment' in Syria has been fairly modest by Russian standards. The sums put into Venezuela are manageable. And the African experiments are extremely low-budget outlays. The attack on Ukraine, of course, was not merely a crime, but also a massive mistake.

Russia can essentially allow itself these costs without undermining the foundations of its economy, especially as, all the while, oil revenues are growing. However, although this Third World War game that the ruling clan is trying to lure Russia into is not high-risk from the point of view of ongoing costs, it is dangerous because it excludes Russia from the ability to take its place in the twenty-first century economy, and dooms it to a slow civilizational death in a historical, technological and social dead-end.

Western countries have excluded us from the global division of labour because we're not regarded as an equal ally or a safe partner. And China, which is steaming ahead in the technological market, certainly doesn't need us as a competitor. On our own, of course, we can't produce even the bare minimum of the technology we need. There are simply too few of us!

In this sense, superpower status is a dangerous myth, and trying to pursue it contradicts the genuine interests of the nation that's trying to come together. But, I repeat, in the near future these problems won't threaten the stability of the regime.

The principal question is not one of cost, but of sense. There was an old Soviet joke: 'Someone asked Armenian Radio: "Could they build socialism in America?" Armenian Radio replied: "Well, they could, but why would they?"' It's the same with the Kremlin's war. Could Russia tactically overcome the West, make itself totally isolated from external influences through autarky (like North Korea) and still extend its control over neighbouring territories? Well, let's say it could; but why would it? We should look not at what would happen if the Kremlin's scheming fails, but what would happen should it succeed. That's where the real disaster would be, because in this logic the Kremlin's victory would mean the defeat of Russia, and vice versa.

So the Kremlin's aim is to demarcate zones of influence with the West (and then with China) so that it can spread its political and military control over certain territories, having put up a new iron curtain. But here's a question: why does a country that has the largest territory in the world (most of it uninhabited), and that's facing an imminent demographic crisis, need new land under its control? After all, controlling a place means that you have to take responsibility for it and spend resources on it, both material and human. Maybe Russia needs more useful mineral resources? But Russia can hardly cope with what it has already. Maybe Russia needs markets for its production of high-tech equipment? But Russia cannot make such equipment (even military equipment) without the cooperation of the same Western world that it wants to shut itself off from with a new iron curtain. And using military means to bring about isolation excludes any such cooperation, anyway. So why is it doing this? What's the secret?

At first glance, the answer is as follows: Russia is ruled today by people with an archaic mentality, people who are mentally stuck not just in the last century but the one before that. They have a primitive, peasant-like understanding of the purpose of politics, that rests, like the Russian peasant's view of the world, on the back of the 'three whales' of Russian folklore.

First, there's the view that any relations with the outside world comprise a zero-sum game: there's always 'us' and 'them', and if 'they' win something then 'we' must have lost by the same amount, and vice versa. There are no shades of colour in this game, there's only black and white. A compromise is just a tactical trap. Alliances just mean military cunning. And in general Russia has only two allies: its army and its navy.

Second, there's the view that holding territory is what's most important of all. That this represents the basis of strength, wealth and influence. The bigger the territory held, the better. The aim of any politician must be to expand their territory. In the framework of this political philosophy, losing any territory is a tragedy, while gaining it is an undoubted positive step. As in the past, the historical significance of any ruler is judged by the amount of territory they've gained or lost.

Third, in the view of the Kremlin strategists, the whole world is divided up into distinct spheres of influence. A sphere of influence is rather like an extension of your territory. It's a space where, even in a limited way, your sovereignty can be projected. It's essential that your foreign and domestic policy

be aimed at extending your sphere of influence. All the functions of the state should be geared towards achieving this.

In the postmodern world, such traditional views have under-
gone a significant rethink. But this news has not yet reached
the Kremlin.

All the main players in modern politics and business are
already operating according to different rules. At the basis of
the new rules is not the theory of the zero-sum game, but the
'win–win' strategy, the so-called 'Nash equilibrium'. This is
the theory that, in complicated systems, no one side in the
relationship can work out a successful strategy if the other
sides don't agree to change their strategies. In other words,
in the modern world no one can achieve substantial success
on their own when playing against everybody else. On the
contrary, it's only when you've learnt to cooperate, agreed the
rules with everyone else, and consented to fulfil them yourself,
that you can noticeably improve your position. The modern
world represents competition within established boundaries
in the interests of all the players. Anyone who wants to play
without these rules is thrown out of the game.

Furthermore, in the twenty-first century, with modern
digital technology, the seizure of territory is certainly not guaranteed to be an advantage. This extra territory could turn out
to be a definite disadvantage, and become too heavy a burden.
The expense of maintaining order in an occupied territory,
involving the cost of social and other infrastructures, as well
as keeping daily life going, could significantly outweigh any
benefit gained.

For some time technologies have been available that allow
an 'economic harvest' to be gathered from 'foreign fields'
without needing to use military force to seize them. The size,
number and high level of education of the population has
become a much more important indicator of economic and
political strength, because this bears witness to a country's
great potential. But Russia's strategists have a real problem

with this. Russia is not only experiencing a declining population, it's also suffering an intellectual decline as the best brains
in the country are being forced out. And the more war games
the country plays, the more intensive this process will become.

In the postmodern world there are no longer clearly defined
dividing lines, and, consequently, no straightforward spheres
of influence. One and the same territory can fall within the
sphere of influence of a number of different countries, at the
same time having an influence on each of them. Everything is
relative; and everything is fluid. There's a constant battle and
constant competition going on in these grey areas. What tends
to happen is that, if someone tries to establish monopolistic
control over some area, they end up losing all influence over it.

The clearest example of such a losing strategy is Russia's
policy towards Ukraine since 2014. Despite having a huge historical advantage, Russia refused to compete with the West for
influence over Ukraine and, literally with its own hands, has
turned it into a hostile state for decades to come, if not forever.
Ukraine is now an exclusion zone between Russia and Europe.

Does this all mean that the principal driving factor of the
Kremlin's policy is stupidity? Only partly. Greed plays an even
bigger role. In reality, the ruling class in Russia doesn't want to
fight. Over the twenty years they've been in power, their representatives have integrated themselves into European life in a
way that's never been done before. They've sent their children,
their wives and their mistresses to Europe; they've acquired real
estate and bank accounts there; they've become the favourite
clients of European bankers and generous patrons of European
politicians. Dozens of university campuses throughout Europe
bear their names. They own fashionable galleries and trading
companies. They don't shy away from innovation, especially
when it's a long way from Russia's borders. Yes, they don't
want Russia to be free; but they're more than ready to make use
of other countries' freedom (and security) in the West. And
therein lies the whole problem.

Possibly to an even greater extent than events in Ukraine, the Magnitsky Act became a trigger point for the Kremlin's crusade against the West. The so-called war against the West carried out in the name of Russia was actually a war of the ruling class for its privileges and, above all, the right to spend its money in the West. That was in its own way a kind of primitive blackmail. Russia didn't attempt to conquer the West (the Kremlin does understand the limits of its capabilities); it just wanted the West to accept its conditions. The principal ones were: don't poke your nose into our business, don't pay attention to what's going on here with human rights and corruption, leave us to gratify our imperial ambitions within the boundaries of the zone of influence of the now defunct USSR, and just let us keep on enjoying your comfortable European lives. But now everything has changed. Putin has dragged Russia into a war that's put the Russian ruling class outside its accustomed place in the international community for many years to come. Now their place is the same as that of the elites of North Korea, Iran and other such marginal countries. That's the mistake – or rather, it's the result – of Putin's evolution from petty thief to fanatic. The interests of the elite have also been thrown overboard.

So how does this match Russia's national interests? The answer is: not at all. How can we understand what those interests are? Let's ask ourselves this question: what do we want to do: bomb Voronezh or revive Voronezh? If we want it bombed, then we don't need anything, and we can go ahead and fight the West. Ah, but if we want to revive it, to make it not like Stalingrad in 1943, but along the lines of Montreal, then we need a lot of things; and all of it is hindered by our confrontation with the West. We need new technology, massive investment, know-how and skilful management, qualitatively improved education and better health care. We need normal competition, without which we have no hope of emerging from stagnation. All of this can be achieved only through integration into the global economy; and integration and war simply don't go together.

Many critics of the current regime go to the other extreme, suggesting that the idea of 'Russia's national interests' is simply an illusion created by propagandists; that there is something dubious about the very phrase. But Russia genuinely does have national interests, and these need to be protected. They do not, though, have anything in common with the narrow, clan interests of the group of thugs from Leningrad, who seized power in Russia and are implementing total militarization of the country. The real national interest for Russia is its fastest possible integration into the global economic system and the restructuring of its political and economic life in such a way that the country can take up a worthy place in this system.

Everything that helps us achieve this goal today is in keeping with Russia's national interests. Everything that hinders the achievement of this goal, or puts off the overdue transformations needed, goes against those interests. The pursuit of a bully's imaginary greatness is insulting to Russia's genuine greatness; there is much to be proud of, and not just the atom bomb.

The Kremlin and its henchmen want to isolate Russia from the West, while at the same time personally integrating into Western life. For this, they need to have the status of a military superpower. But Russia's national interests are diametrically opposed to this. We need to remove the country's isolation, while, on the other hand, isolating all those who use the threat of war to maintain their feudal privileges, including the right to steal money from the country with impunity and spend it in the West. They want Russia to be closed off, so that they can steal and deceive forever. We want Russia to be open, so that this can never happen again.

14

The Historical Choice:
Muscovy or Gardarika (which has nothing to do with Gaidar)?

Will Russia be an empire or a nation-state? Will the focus be on building a better life for itself, or will it waste its time trying to create yet another utopia of universal proportions? Whatever the situation is, a crucial question for future generations will be about the centralization of power in Russia. Should the Russian political system remain strictly centralized, with most (if not all) authority concentrated in the hands of the federal government in Moscow? Or should it be decentralized (even if only artificially)? And, even if it takes enormous effort, should a multitude of places across the country be empowered to make certain political decisions, depending on their level of competence?

Either variant is possible within the liberal and democratic model. Simply turning away from the authoritarian system doesn't remove the question. In both theory and practice a democratic state can be strongly centralized – Britain and France are examples of this – or it can be largely decentralized, such as in the USA and Germany. We will have to choose which would suit Russia best, taking into consideration our cultural heritage, and the particulars of the new, unique historic tasks that will lie before us. This is not a simple or clear-cut choice, not least because it goes against a deeply rooted political tradition.

Matters are made more complicated because centralism is the sacred cow of Russian political mentality. Attacking this would be fraught with risks. In each of the three previous incarnations of its civilization – Muscovy, the Empire and the USSR – Russia was a hyper-centralized state. The tradition was laid down by Muscovy, intensified by Peter the Great's Empire, and taken to its extreme by the Communist empire. And neither in the 1990s, nor in the first decade of the twenty-first century, did anything change significantly. So for the past 500 years of history, the movement has been only towards greater centralization, and never the other way. You could say that, despite the many changes of eras, Russia is still Muscovy.

Paradoxically, centralism as a political principle is so deep-rooted in the mass consciousness that the idea unites both the supporters and the opponents of the current Russian regime. Among the latter group, there are fanatics who believe just as strongly in concentrating power in the hands of a national government in Moscow as do the apologists for the regime. Even though the motives of these political forces are completely different, they both relate to the idea of decentralization with the same scepticism and suspicion.

For the clan that rules Russia, this is a question of the type of control that they can exert over the situation, a matter of maintaining the political and economic status quo. For them, hyper-centralization is a tool for suppressing any challenges or local grievances that threaten the established political order. Naturally, for them, centralism is the main means of maintaining the stability of the regime. They are totally dependent on the centralized apparatus for repression and for the propaganda needed to carry out its work effectively. It's also the way in which they maintain control over the resources that are essential for keeping this apparatus going.

For the opposition, centralism is a guaranteed way of defending citizens from the despotism of local elites, whom they see as strongholds of reaction. The results of an experiment to introduce the first steps towards local self-governance that was carried out by the young Tsar Ivan IV (later to be known as 'the Terrible') have still not been wiped from the historical memory. In the regions, power was seized from the governor by the tsar's agents, the so-called 'leatherlungs', whose excesses were even crueller than people were used to from the tsar's governor. As a result, the experiment had to be stopped in its initial phase.

Perhaps this is why many of the ideologists of Russian liberalism supported centralism, because they felt that decentralizing power in Russia would inevitably lead to incidents like the one in Kushchovskaya in 2010, when local gangsters killed twelve people. They feared that this could create a kind of confederacy of such semi-lawless principalities, each run by a criminal gang's authoritarian micro-regime. They believed that the only thing that could prevent this disastrous situation would be to give the dominant role to a 'progressive' central authority, the federal government, which would be controlled by the 'correct' political forces – that is, the victorious Westernizing liberals.

Therefore, just like the reactionaries, certain Russian liberals speak out in favour of maintaining strict centralization. Their principal area of disagreement is simply over who should control this united centre, and what signals the centre should send out to the regions. Those loyal to the regime believe that centralized power will guarantee stability and prevent change, while others in this group of liberals and democrats think that the centre should ensure that necessary reforms are implemented from the top down throughout the country.

It would be possible to consider the arguments from these liberals in favour of centralism to be wholly convincing, were it not for one thing: in a huge country like Russia, centralism will, sooner or later, inevitably lead to authoritarianism.

As long as there is a high degree of centralization of power, it's impossible to maintain a workable model of democracy in the country over a long period. However liberal the centralized power of the victorious progressive forces is at the start, it will quickly cease to be so and will once again become authoritarian.

There's an obvious reason why keeping hyper-centralization in Russia ends up merely replicating the authoritarian model. Centralism presupposes the necessity for the constant redistribution of resources within a huge country (otherwise there'd be no material base). This means that enormous financial flows have to be serviced, and a massive bureaucratic structure is needed for this. And this bureaucracy, in turn, hangs over a society that has neither the means to control it nor ways of defending itself against it.

The chain is simple: centralization; redistribution of resources; a huge structure to service this; suppression of civil society.

In other words (and this is very important), in Russian conditions centralization inevitably breeds autocracy, and vice versa.

Whatever innovative ideas the revolutionary centrists might have had when they came to power in Russia, they slid into (and will continue to slide into) the same well-worn historical rut: the imposition of change from above; the creation of a huge structure of centralized power; the necessity to focus resources on servicing this structure; the move to turn this structure into a force that lords it over society; the formation of an authoritarian (at best) regime; the need for a new revolution.

So how do you break out of this vicious circle, and how do you get away from the authoritarian nature of this centralized power without becoming the hostage of the local criminal gangs?

The answer seems pretty obvious. You decentralize power while strengthening society's control, providing balance and creating a separation of powers; you allow for a strong opposition that is guaranteed a place in maintaining control over the authorities; and you have an independent media.

But how do you achieve all this in a country where, for the last 500 years at least, there has been virtually no such political experience?

Decentralization of the political system is perhaps the single most important political task facing the coalition of forces that, in practice, not in theory, is trying to bring about the democratization of Russia.

This is an extremely difficult task. It's impossible to leap across this chasm in one bound and land immediately in a decentralized paradise. There are already too many archaic layers in the Russian political system and it's too difficult to bring them all down to a single common denominator. Furthermore, there's a great risk that, in chasing after this ideal, you lose sight of reality and end up falling into the chasm. At the same time, though, you can't avoid making the jump. Because sooner or later, all these archaisms will tear the country apart at the seams.

So we have to immediately attack on two fronts: prepare the ground for a tectonic shift, while taking temporary, compromise measures. These may be imperfect, but they'll still go some way towards solving the problem.

What can serve as a template for this new system? Strange as it may seem, the answer can be found in Russia's distant past, even further back than the usual point from which Russian statehood is usually measured: the Tsardom of Muscovy.

Today, the united forces of reaction are pushing us into the past, and they see their ideal in the state that was created by the princes of Muscovy. But our history didn't begin with the victory over the Tatars and the creation of Muscovy that followed this. There was another Rus' before this. It was a country of self-governing and totally independent towns: Gardarika ('the land of towns', in the language of the Viking traders of the time). And even though these towns have been lost in the endless expanses of Russian civilization, it's Gardarika that we need today in place of Muscovy as the fundamentally different state structure, as an alternative to the harshness of centralization.

Towns and cities have always been the cornerstone for the development of European civilization, and to this day they remain the principal places for the growth of the new global civilization. But now we're talking not just about cities, but about mega-cities – vast cities where millions of people live in close proximity to each other. As the fundamentally new system of social organization, it's these mega-cities that have become the engines of global technological, economic and even cultural change.

Strategically, even in the medium-term historical perspective, Muscovy, with its single dominating centre for taking political decisions, should be transformed into a mega-city based on political multicentrism. Ideally, the basis of the state structure in Russia should be a political union of mega-cities. This would greatly broaden the political class, taking it beyond the Moscow Ring Road.

The fundamental difference between the modern world and that of centuries past is that today there are far fewer centres of development. Development is now concentrated in the biggest mega-cities, where there's a sufficient concentration of people and infrastructure. A mega-city is a place where people live in relatively close proximity to each other, and whose centre can be reached in less than an hour. The surrounding area then becomes the territory for servicing these centres of growth. In Russia, the emphasis going forward should be placed on expanding mega-cities that currently have a population of 3–5 million, to reach up to 15–20 million.

This is less of a technical question than a political one. How many of these centres do we need, and how many can we allow ourselves? This is the essence of proper strategic planning (if, of course, we want to control the direction in which we are heading and not merely go with the flow of time).

In my opinion, there can be no more than twenty such centres in Russia. We simply don't have a large enough population for more than that. In the future, these metropolises will become territorial centres, the capitals of a new structural organization. We might call them 'lands'.

We're talking about new economic and political entities. These will be the building blocks of the new Russia, constructed from the bottom up, and not from the top down, as has been the practice up until now. This new network of 'lands' will eventually replace the existing system of oblasts and republics.

I am convinced that, whatever happens, at some point in our historical development we will have to change today's territorial and state delineation of Russia, which has its roots partly in the country's ancient history and partly in the results of spontaneous decisions and passing interests.

It may well be that we have to abandon the territorial division of guberniyas and oblasts, which we've known for nearly 300 years. These divisions arose in a historically natural fashion, randomly, during endless Russian colonial expansion. They underpin uneven development, and formalize the peaceful coexistence between the rich regions (each of which could become a separate European state) and the poorer areas, which survive only thanks to subsidies from the centre and are totally unprepared for an independent existence, not just economically but in the wider cultural meaning of the word as well.

Nowhere in the world are all regions set up on an equal footing. There's always a contrast between the leaders and the outsiders. But everything is relative. You won't last long if you try to harness a postindustrial steed together with a nervous tribal-society donkey to the same cart of a modern postindustrial nation-state. The developmental levelling up of different regions is essential politically, raising the status of the outsiders to that of the leaders. Improving the most backward regions that are not currently able to fulfil the political functions of a subject of the Federation (and, indeed, who are not even really such 'subjects' at all) is a very difficult but essential task.

But you can't do this on the spur of the moment. First, you have to develop the mega-cities as potential (future) administrative political and economic centres so that they can carry out their new role. We have to begin by creating a proper, quality university, that will set the level of the future mega-city. And this will take a long time.

So what can we do more immediately? If we simply rely on the possible growth of the mega-cities, we may never live to see the bright new future. The project for the deep restructuring of Russia's territorial state system could take a decade, if not longer. And if throughout these years the power structure remains as centralized as it is now, there will be no possibility of breaking out of the prison of authoritarianism and economic backwardness that Russia currently finds itself in. This means that, at the same time as the new system is being rolled out, we need to reform the existing system – the 'temporary solution'.

How should we approach the current reality? History has known two main ways of effectively decentralizing power: self-governance and federalism. Neither of these has been studied in depth in Russia. Even though they're both mentioned in the Constitution, they've never been put into practice, and so they remain there as mere false decorations of the political system. We can merely guess at how genuine self-governance and real federalism would work in Russia.

Russia has never really been a genuine federal state. The idea of the federation was simply a political formula to legitimize the limited autonomy of the colonies in their relation to the metropolis. The model of a federation has never worked in Russia, and no one can even be sure that it would work there. It was effective in the USSR only so much as backing up the 'show' federal model of Soviet power was the highly centralized machinery of the Party's power (the real deep state), to which the federative principle did not apply.

Self-governance has fairly deep roots in Russia, and in the pre-Soviet period it played an important supporting role in rural areas at the lower levels of governance of the Empire. From the mid-nineteenth century, more complicated methods of self-governance began to develop, such as the *zemstvo*. But in the Soviet period all self-governance was wiped out, and the tradition was lost. Nothing of its kind has been created in the post-Soviet period. So any moves towards self-governance will have to start from scratch.

Nevertheless, we do have something that could be used as a starting point, and something that could be used for careful political refinement. I see the pre-emptive development of local self-governance as the key condition that would make it difficult to slide into the well-worn rut of authoritarianism. Developing federalism – that would be an extra supporting factor. This is because it would be relatively easy to build public oversight over structures of power that exist close by, and a democratic tradition could be created on this basis.

The basic essentials needed for developing local self-governance are a protected budget and clearly defined areas of competence. The concept of 'joint (or mixed) competence' is a tricky one. It's a grey area, where the centre always wins. Self-governance, of course, means there must be responsibility. This is a closed circle of political technology: a clearly defined area of competence, its own revenue base and administration by elected officials who answer to the electorate for the results of their work. The electorate themselves then carry the responsibility for their own mistakes, and can't blame them on a higher level of government.

Clearly, like people, regions are not all the same, and in a massive country like Russia you can't avoid a redistribution of resources. But this must be done transparently, by a united fund for regional development, and not secretively through murky line items of the overall federal budget. So the question of transparency has to be decided separately.

Access to subsidies has to be fair and must stimulate local development. Subsidies must not be used for political trade-offs, or as a means of paying for 'voting the right way'.

As local self-governance rapidly develops, it will help change the rotten stick of the authorities into a pyramid, with self-governance as the foundation of this pyramid. This means that today's whole system will be turned upside down. People must learn to solve problems at the level where they happen. No democracy in the world exists without this foundation. The rules are simple: it's your competence, your budget, your elected leaders.

At the top of the pyramid we have the central authorities. In practice, they should be secondary to local authorities, complementary to their work, and not the other way round. The central authorities are not there to solve the local problems of the self-governing authorities, but to establish the rules of the game and make sure they are rigorously observed. If they are not, then the foundations of the system will begin to crack, and the same criminal gangs will take over once again.

Furthermore, the central authorities are there to solve national issues. To ensure they can do this, they must have their own protected areas of competence and sufficient resources, including a central budget. They have to be strong enough to ensure that, in the field, the rules and order are adhered to; but these have to be sufficiently kept in check so that the central authorities aren't tempted to 'privatize' the field and devour the competence of the local self-governing authorities.

But here, an extra problem arises. If the central authorities are too weak, they won't be able to hold the country together. But if they're too strong, then they'll overpower local self-governance and crush it.

In order to regulate the power of the central authorities, and to ensure that they cannot break the established order by de facto seizing power from the local self-governing bodies, an artificially created extra, horizontal, barrier has to be set up from within. This is to guarantee the separation of powers. This extra regulator, built in to the central authorities, is federalism. In such an enormous country as Russia, this is an essential element to make sure that the balance between the central authority and self-governance is maintained.

Unfortunately, the very meaning of the word 'federalism' is today besmirched by many years of Soviet propaganda.

Federalism is a specific way of organizing state power, where, along with the vertical division (the classic division of powers), there is an additional horizontal division, the so-called 'constitutional covenant'. This makes it possible for these two levels of state power to operate on one territory, with full autonomy (that is, establishing their own rules), in one or more areas of competence.

The federalism that I'm talking about here has nothing in common with today's false federalism. In the future, it will be associated with the mega-cities, which will be the centres of the new subjects of the state. But we need to start by changing the relations within the framework of the existing territorial divisions of the state.

In the future, mega-cities will become the capitals of the 'lands', which will enjoy all the necessary administrative and political attributes of local capitals, as well as tightly attached judicial systems, military districts and so on. The lands will have their own legislation within the scope of their competence. It's possible today more or less to predict what the list of the lands and their capitals will be, by looking at how individual regions are developing. They can already be prepared for their new role, including by purposely and systematically consolidating and enlarging the existing subjects of the Federation.

Only a three-dimensional system will be able to survive in Russia, with a strong central government, a mega-city as a regional centre and strong local self-governance. If one or other of the links in this chain collapses, or if the system flattens out and stops being three-dimensional, then it will inevitably return to traditional authoritarianism, or run the risk of the state disintegrating into tiny pieces. The foundation of all three elements must be self-governance. And the foundation of self-governance must be a protected local budget and competence.

The old model of running Russia is Muscovy, a country of a single city-state. But for Russia to become a modern state, the new model has to be Gardarika, a country of multiple cities that take power into their own hands. Gardarika versus Muscovy. Ultimately, this is the argument upon which the fate of Russia will depend.

15

The Political Choice: Democracy or a Return to the Terror of the Oprichnina?

I f we stop to think about it, why do we need democracy? Why do we need this system of power based on regular general elections and the separation of the branches of power? Why is it necessary at all? And why specifically in Russia?

The answer is far from clear. Or, to be more precise, it's far from clear for everyone. The liberally minded Russian opposition tends to believe that everyone understands that democracy is a good thing; and those who don't understand this are just pretending they don't. But this is a serious delusion.

Even in the most liberal of circles, you come across fierce antidemocrats who are convinced that democracy is merely for the chosen ones. And in the non-liberal sphere, opponents of democracy dominate in Russia; it's just that not everyone speaks out on this topic, many preferring to remain silent. So the question as to whether Russia really should become a democratic state or not remains an open one.

The simplest thing to do would be to write off this 'demo-scepticism' as resulting from closed-mindedness or a lack of culture; but it's much more complicated than that.

First of all, there are quite a few highly educated intellectuals among the opponents of democracy; they're not all just common people who've been duped by the regime.

Second, there are plenty of genuine problems in the way modern democracy works, and these have discredited it in the eyes of people who have a wide variety of political views.

Third (and perhaps most importantly), Russia has only a tiny experience of democracy, whereas, at the other end of the scale, its experience of authoritarian rule is huge; inertia has instilled into many people much more trust in this system, which they know.

And we have to remember that Russia is an 'atypical dictatorship'. Russian authoritarianism is unique in its own way, and has demonstrated its ability to modernize time and again. Throughout its evolution, the Russian political system has formulated its own original answer to the challenges of history, which can be summed up as a 'permanent oprichnina'. This system is not as primitive as many might think it is.

The essence of the oprichnina is the division of power into an external and an internal state, where the internal controls the external and is a hidden political force.

First established by Ivan the Terrible, the oprichnina has gone through multiple transformations. At different times, this internal state has been called by different names (such as 'the imperial court', 'the Communist Party', or the 'Lake cooperative'). But in essence it has remained as it always was: while the regular state has existed, an additional network of informal power above all the usual laws and institutions was laid atop it, one that hasn't been identified by any laws. It's the power of the overseers, standing above the law and living by their own privileges. It's a specific kind of Russian eternal Middle Ages. It changes and constantly adapts to new circumstances, but never, ever, fully disappears.

The image of some magical force of these Middle Ages has become an integral part of the people's historic memory; they remember that any attempt to escape from this paradigm has ended with some kind of time of troubles.

This image doesn't need to be helped by propaganda. It's the first association that springs into the mass Russian political consciousness. So the renewed enthusiasm for Stalinism that many talk about today shouldn't be regarded simplistically as just people being brainwashed by television. It has deep roots, not to mention that a significant segment of the population continues to feel positive about Stalin and the methods he used for he used running the country, and did so even during the 'democracy rampage'. Of course, this part of society didn't always behave as aggressively and as shamelessly as they do today, but they haven't changed their principles in the slightest.

At the base of this enduring sympathy is a belief in the effectiveness of Stalin's way of ruling, especially when it was necessary to quickly mobilize limited resources so as to achieve a specific result.

A significant part of Russian society is convinced even today that Stalinism has great potential for modernization, and this is a reality that cannot be ignored. Well before Putin appeared on the scene, there was talk in Russia about Stalin, and even Ivan the Terrible, as being efficient managers, but no one really paid any attention to it, dismissing it as nonsense. Wrongly, as it turns out. Here we need proper arguments, not emotions. Up to now there's been more of the latter than the former.

The substantive objections that the liberal part of society puts forward against Stalinism and in favour of democracy are largely based on two principles, the ethical and the economic. The ethical principle talks of 'the price paid' – the millions of lives lost to win Stalin's 'victory'. The economic principle maintains that half a century later the country broke up, and a significant reason was that we had clearly fallen behind democratic countries in terms of economic development.

The Stalinists usually fend off the ethical argument by saying that democracy too has not always been whiter than white, that democratic revolutions frequently result in huge numbers of victims. And to the economic argument they answer that the fatal lag in the economy took place in the post-Stalin period.

Some people may feel that the Stalinists are right, and that the potential of the totalitarian society for modernization was truly unlimited. But this impression swiftly disappears when you take into account the long historical perspective.

It appears that Peter the Great and Stalin both achieved some success in the economy once they had the country under their control. But towards the end of their lives, just one or two generations after they began their reforms (between twenty and forty years), stagnation set in that was impossible to resist. And the roots of this stagnation clearly lay in the period of great victories. Ultimately, it could be seen that these 'victories', as consequences of revolution, turned out to be the reasons for the backwardness of the system. Thanks to the authoritarian nature of Russia's modernization, the country developed from revolution to revolution along the lines of 'one step forward, two steps back'. And as the centuries passed, the upheavals, like a pendulum, swung back and forth ever stronger. There's no point in making the usual comparison between authoritarian modernization and some archaic past; we need to compare how effective authoritarian and non-authoritarian modernization has been over long periods of time.

In places where democracy ruled, development happened much more evenly, with fewer swings of the historical pendulum. And over long periods of time this gave society a massive head start. The people's patience wasn't exhausted under the yoke of autocracy, nor did it explode into a bloody civil war, or turn into appalling apathy witnessing the endless rule of gerontocratic leaders. One set of politicians just peacefully took the place of another, one political course was exchanged for another, and society merely tacked against the wind of the various hardships that life threw up.

Again and again, Russia has been put in the position of trying to catch up, despite all the sacrifices that were placed on the altar of authoritarian modernization. This is where Russia is now once more. Strategically speaking, if we take a long historical perspective, if we look far into the distance instead of simply looking under our feet, we can see that, for Russia, there is no alternative to democracy. Otherwise, sooner or later another swing of the pendulum of revolution will simply destroy Russia as a state. And a massive swing of this pendulum can be avoided only with the help of democracy. But the question is, what sort of democracy does our country need, and how can we build it with the minimum of cost?

This task has to be solved on two levels at once. First, Russia has to construct a democratic foundation, to do what was done long ago in Western Europe. But just catching up with the West isn't enough. We have to take into account the new challenges that have arisen. Modern Western democracy is experiencing serious difficulties and is now seeking answers to these problems. There's no point in our first creating the democracy of the nineteenth century (which is what everyone is trying to do) and then trying to reshape it for today.

The classic form of democracy no longer works anywhere. Its time has passed. In the information age, the methods of political mobilization that were invented in the middle of the nineteenth century are both pointless and useless. Every day we see how the old system of political parties is stagnating and is no longer capable of fulfilling its function. In Russia we must, from the start, build a democracy for the twenty-first century, leaping at one go over two steps and proving correct the words of the Evangelist, that those who are last can be first.

What does 'creating a democratic foundation' mean in Russia? There are hundreds of definitions of democracy in the world and dozens of different theories. I don't intend to put forward a fundamentally new version, nor will I just repeat certain banalities. One way or another, the type of society that will be considered as democratic is going to be the one where society has the last word when it comes to taking political decisions – the whole of society, including its minorities. Not just a part of society, which for some particular reason has the right to vote, such as by material wealth, education, ethnicity and so on, but the whole adult and legally competent population of the country.

In this sense I will always be suspicious of democracy in countries where there are too many people who are not treated as citizens, whatever the historical background to this might be.

Let me just point out right away that I'm not talking here about restoring democracy, but about the creation of a social structure that Russia will have for the first time in its history. The right of society to have the decisive voice has never been known here, not even in the most liberal, long-gone days (including the short period between the February and Bolshevik Revolutions in 1917 – let's not confuse anarchy with democracy as a means of organization), or in the more turbulent times of recent years, such as the 1990s.

It is essential that there be no blatant examples of political repression, but this is not of itself a sufficient sign of democracy.

At the end of 1993, after the armed conflict with the supporters of the Supreme Soviet, the Russian political system was deliberately constructed in such a way as to remove the figure of the president from the declared – but never implemented – separation of powers. In this sense, the Constitution of post-Communist Russia hardly changed from the constitutional laws of the autocratic Empire. As a result, this led to the total deterioration of statehood in Russia: power became concentrated in the hands of the president and his circle, which led to the establishment of a neo-totalitarian regime.

So the fundamental question for the creation of democracy in Russia is this: how do we bring the supreme authority into a system where there is separation of powers, lock it into a method of checks and balances, place the deep state under the control of society and, indeed, do away with its 'sacred' significance entirely? This is a purely institutional task, which can – and must be – solved through constitutional law within the framework of general political reform.

Perhaps in current circumstances the best way to solve this is by switching to a parliamentary democracy. Whatever happens, Russia's political institutions (whatever names they go by) must not be allowed to rise above all the other branches of power and gain an authority that is not balanced out by that of the other branches. This is the only way in which democracy's 'golden share' can remain in society's hands, and won't be seized by gangs close to the supreme leader.

But even if, in practice, Russia were able to carry out such deep institutional reform, would this make the country a successful and democratic state?

The answer isn't simple. Democratic? Yes. Successful? No. The reason for this ambiguity lies in the systemic challenges and glitches that democracy faces everywhere today – not just in Russia, but around the world, including in the West, democracy's *alma mater*. First of all, the electoral mechanisms, which are based on the work of party machines, are no longer as relevant as before. In the developed informational society, political parties have ceased to be the only, or even the main, instruments for politically motivating the population.

Nowadays, small, mobile groups of activists have become the way of doing this. They may not have broad representation among the mass of the population, but with sufficient resources they are capable of quickly establishing contact with people through modern media channels, and guiding them in the direction that they want.

This means that the possible sources of support for political action in today's world are widely differentiated, and it is difficult to establish public control over them even in societies with reliable democratic traditions and stable state institutions.

The meaning of these changes in a functioning democracy is ambiguous. On the one hand, they make the political system more dynamic, adaptive and (naturally) more open. But, on the other hand, they open up wide possibilities for manipulating public opinion, thereby creating an unhealthy populism, and in this way they destroy the very essence of the electoral process. For now, it's not clear how to teach democracy to work in these fundamentally new conditions. One thing is very clear though: if the best we can do in Russia is simply to build 'yesterday's democracy', then, despite all the efforts and sacrifices made, it won't work and the whole project will collapse even before it's started. And the very idea of democracy will be even more discredited.

This means that Russia must aim to be not only a democracy, but the most advanced democratic society possible, using the newest political technologies to make this happen. One of the problems is that we don't really have anywhere to observe how others have done this. We are doomed once again to become a country of social and political invention. Yet again! And this isn't because we would want it to be so. It's simply that other countries have time on their side; they can use the political capital they already have, but we can't do that in Russia. One way or the other, we have to build a democratic system virtually from scratch, in a completely new way, at our own risk, trusting to our own intuition rather than basing it on the experience of others. Certain liberal Westernized Russians don't appreciate this. They put too much hope in the approaches that have been developed in Europe.

In addition to the 'compulsory programme' of democracy, which boils down primarily to the competent implementation of institutional reforms needed to destroy the Russian system of autocracy through the separation of powers, Russia is facing a huge democratic 'free programme', the success of which will depend to a large extent on how well this is executed. This programme will not be simple. The level of difficulty of the democratic system should be suitable for the level of difficulty of modern society.

I'll allow myself a comparison. The same principle operates in both a small trading enterprise and a gigantic international corporation. The shareholders make the main decisions based on a majority of votes. But the manner in which the majority exercise their rights differs in each firm. A gigantic corporation operating in several different industries can't operate in the same way that a small shop does. It has in place a multitude of special mechanisms to guard against mistakes that might be made by the majority (which happen quite often in practice). These are mechanisms that guarantee the rights of the majority, but prevent them from halting the work of the enterprise and abusing these rights.

The same is true in a state. Democracy is a very complicated system, perhaps even more complicated than authoritarianism, and one that is always tailor-made for a particular country at a particular moment in time.

Creating such a system for a huge, territorially and culturally diverse country like Russia, with its huge differences in nature and climate, is not easy. This gives rise to the idea that we must experiment with different parliamentary systems, allow asymmetry and, of course, devolve as many decisions as possible to the lowest level – we must decentralize everything that can be decentralized. We have to start from the idea that there's never been a genuine, classic party system in Russia, and there never will be. Therefore, we have to build the electoral mechanism around something else – something that's now replacing traditional parties.

We have to prepare for all of this now, opening up a discussion on the political format of the future Russian democracy, and not leaving the search for a solution until later – because there won't be time 'later'. And this shouldn't be just empty incantations about the benefits of democracy, or idle chatter about its general principles.

This must be a discussion about the details, involving specialists and as wide a group of interested parties as possible. After all, the authoritarian devil hides in the democratic detail. This is what we saw in the very best Constitution in 1993. We mustn't allow ourselves to repeat that mistake.

16

The Economic Choice: Monopoly or Competition?

Y ou have only to mention the word 'monopoly' – and, even more so, 'competition' – and all those who aren't connected in any way to economics or business imme- diately lose interest, and sigh, 'There you go again!' A natural monopoly, unnatural privileges . . . 'How much more are you going to bang on about it?! Everyone knows that monopoly is bad and competition is good.' Is there really any reason to keep beating a dead horse? But it turns out there is a reason. Monopoly and competition don't refer to the economy. Well, to be more precise, they do, of course, refer to the economy, but only slightly. More significantly they refer to a lifestyle and a way of thinking. In essence, we're talking here about two different ways of looking at the whole social structure. So it's about politics, the society and also ideology.

There's a law that links several interconnected social domains. It runs like this: if there's a monopoly in the economy, then sooner or later you'll have authoritarianism in politics, paternalism in social relations and some sort of totalitarianism in ideology. This happens because monopoly and all the social and political conditions related to it are the result of certain dominating sociocultural factors. This is particularly characteristic of Russian society. We can take away the prospect of monopoly only if we manage to change these dominating factors; otherwise, we'll simply swap one monopoly for another.

Monopoly and competition do not sit at opposite ends of the spectrum. They are not totally opposed to each other, as many simplistically assume. At the same time, they are doomed to be in permanent conflict with one another. But you can never completely remove either monopoly or competition. Each is really just a way of combating chaos. They are ways of organizing social space. One has some good points; so does the other.

For example, let's take the state's monopoly over the legalized use of force. Nowadays, this is the generally recognized legal norm, but this has not always been the case. But judging by the expanding number of private armies such as the Wagner Group, from a future historical perspective, who knows?

In a practical sense, there are two ways of fighting chaos. There's the tough way – clamping down on it with the help of the hierarchy of power (the vertical way) – and there's the softer way: using the rules of the road to guide it in the right direction.

So competition shouldn't be confused with a war of all against all. Organized competition, like monopoly, is called upon to struggle against this war, but using different methods.

To a certain extent, monopolies are always natural. The consolidation of capital and the associated increase in production are caused primarily by the need to increase labour productivity. In any case, until recently, labour productivity increased as the business grew larger. This is due to a number of reasons, not least because within a large enterprise it's easier to form work patterns and implement a system of control that allows for the mistakes of the workers to be corrected. Of course, such factors as the concentration of resources and the stress tolerance related to this are also significant.

Even the most progressive start-ups consider it a true mark of the success of what they've created when they are bought out by a transnational giant. But at the same time, as a monopoly develops, labour productivity begins to fall away, because there are fewer incentives to improve the production process. Why change it if it's not broken? As a result, sooner or later any giant company becomes less efficient.

So expanding a business is positive when it's done in a controlled way, but negative if it becomes uncontrolled. The easiest way to establish control over a monopoly is to develop competition; in other words, to put big businesses in competition with each other, providing this is kept within the boundaries of the established rules. The responsibility for this, as the arbiter, lies with the state.

The approaches to this question are generally well known and universal. Once a monopoly controls more than 30 per cent of the market, it should be placed under observation to ensure against abuse of the system. If it goes over 60 per cent of the market, measures have to be taken to reduce the profitability of the monopoly, by stimulating other producers of goods and services. This is rather like a perpetual battle against buildings becoming iced over: you have constantly to break off the largest icicles.

Monopolization in markets is similar to fighting herpes: you can never defeat it, but you can keep it in a suppressed state if you have political and economic immunity that operates effectively. But unlike herpes, expansion is not an illness but natural evolution, and this has to be utilized.

The ways in which this is done can vary. It doesn't have to be the straight-down-the-line approach of Europe or the USA. For example, South Korea is the home of the Samsung Corporation, a monopoly company. The government provides it with protection, as it were. But this same government also sets rigid guidelines, such that no less than 60 per cent of Samsung's output can be produced for export. If these conditions are not met, the company faces serious sanctions. You could call this 'competition replacement therapy'. It is a very different approach, but it solves the question of control over a monopoly.

The situation changes drastically when a private monopoly becomes state-owned, in the hands of a state corporation. In this case, neither market forces nor replacement therapy will work, and any competition will be incinerated with administrative napalm.

No private enterprise can possibly compete with the consolidated power of the state when the state is both owner and controller. If anyone doesn't know how this works, they should study carefully the garbage and construction businesses of the Russian Prosecutor General. There can also be no question of one government official being able to effectively control another (and, by default, all the leaders of state corporations are *ipso facto* the biggest of government officials). In Russia, everyone witnessed how even the slightest hint of such control can finish with the example of the Ulyukaev affair. Alexey Ulyukaev ended up in the meat-grinder, at the place where they make 'Sechin's sausages'.

In Russia, the idea of monopoly has deep historic roots, which is why it has so many supporters. Nearly all industry was founded on the state's initiative, with the participation of the state and under the state's control (even if that initiative was corruptly motivated by the future owner). Monopoly was the main instrument for the industrialization of the state. And after the Bolshevik Revolution it became its sole instrument for industrialization. The principle of monopoly was taken to absurd lengths, far further than it had ever been taken before in any large global economy. In the end, this monopoly was what killed off the USSR, because it made its economy inefficient and uncompetitive.

After the collapse of the USSR, Russia significantly freed itself from the grip of the monopoly. But this was only for a very short period, and it wasn't able to organize proper competition. The economic and political institutions of post-Communist society couldn't cope with the enormous challenges of the time. As a result, society went into a tailspin, which resulted in exactly the kind of war of all against all that monopoly and competition are supposed to defend against. At the start of this century, the strategic mistake was made to restart the monopoly, instead of continuing to rebuild the field of competition. But this turned out to be a very particular monopoly, the like of which Russia had never experienced.

In this authoritarian regime, which is corrupt from top to bottom and bereft of any ideology (in place of which they use some sort of rusty paper-clips), the monopoly has become nothing more than a way by which the clans can get rich, by sucking up to power. The regime uses monopolies to reward the clans for their political loyalty. So monopolies have become the most convertible currency of post-Communist Russia. Instead of handing out cash, it hands out monopolies. It started with oil and gas extraction, then spread to road tolls, and then to anything and everything. Now, according to the latest reports, it's even spread to toilets. It's not surprising that this vital sector of the economy went to the family of the former Prosecutor General, Yuri Chaika; after all, it's right up his street.

To be fair, it should be pointed out that even before this there were few preconditions in Russia for the successful development of competition. So creating the conditions now for competition would be a tricky task for any government, including the one to which it will fall to build the new Russia once the present regime evaporates into nothing. Such preconditions usually include a readiness to cooperate, a broad base of trust, and other attributes of a bourgeois society; everything that's included in Max Weber's code of Protestant ethics. Unfortunately, no such ethical code has emerged in Russia.

Despite the common perception that Russians have a collectivist mind from birth, even researchers with diametrically opposed views on the fate of Russia have pointed out that a pathological individualism (what the philosopher Ivan Ilin called 'federalism') is characteristic of Russian people.

The most severe measures have always been employed in order to crush this eternally excessive Russian individualism, including the ubiquitous use of monopolies. To a great extent, over time monopolies in Russia have become a historically determined way of survival due to the significant suppression of initiative. The well-known Russian notion of forced *sobornost* [a term without parallel in other languages, but described as 'a spiritual community of many people living together' – Tr.], was merely a reaction to the inability to gently wipe out individualism with the aid of general rules. But historically, even this method has had its limits: after a while it simply stops working.

As a way of dealing with chaos, competition is now preferred to monopoly almost everywhere. But in Russia, with its difficult cultural heritage, competition simply failed to develop sufficiently to be able to carry out what it's meant to do. At every turn it came up against an autocratic leader who tried to solve problems that arose by using a monopoly. And the result? It was totally ineffective and cost huge sums of money.

Peter the Great created a centralized industry that was almost totally dependent on the state. The Bolsheviks carried this tendency to its logical conclusion, leaving standing only a state-planned economy. It's not worth dwelling on the cost of this, or on the result. It was always a crude, harsh and uneconomic way of doing things, but it carried on working for centuries.

Why doesn't this work now? Because when you have a society with a developed system of information, monopoly as the basic way of regulating the social sphere is outdated.

When all societal relationships have become much more complicated, and success depends increasingly on the actions of a solitary individual or small groups, it becomes virtually impossible to support the dynamic development of society by way of a monopoly. Russia has no choice but to move from a monopoly economy to a competitive economy. But achieving this is no easy task.

The advantages of competition may not be very obvious, although it's abundantly clear from experience that competition beats monopoly. The experience of economic development in nearly all large economic systems – the USA, Russia, China – shows this to be the case. The death of the Soviet system is in many ways on the consciences of those who failed to recognize in time the fatal flaws of the monopoly. I would even dare to suggest that, had the Soviet system evolved along the lines proposed by Alexander Shelepin and Alexei Kosygin, rather than in the way championed by Leonid Brezhnev and Mikhail Suslov, and had Kosygin's reforms been carried out in full, then the end of the USSR might have been different.

But it's less a question of what's abundantly clear from experience, rather than the basic principle. Competition is simply a more efficient way of running any area of society. Its very potential outweighs that of a monopoly. Competition is an individual's game, organized according to general and strictly observed rules. These encompass both sides of the coin: there's the players' freedom of action and their ability to choose the direction in which they move, even as, at the same time, they previously agreed on rules that no individual can change or simply ignore. In other words, the main thing about competition is its rules, which, by observing them, give each player a wide freedom of choice.

In a monopoly, on the other hand, the main thing is orders. Under a monopoly, only one player is free: the person who singlehandedly establishes both the rules and the direction of travel. It's specifically because it encompasses the two elements – order and freedom of choice – that competition is more efficient than monopoly. Psychologically, it's competition and not monopoly that suits man's natural instincts more closely.

From this understanding of competition, it follows that its key features are the drawing up and then the observation of the rules. There can be no competition if some are more equal than others. But this isn't enough.

There has to be equal and fair access to the process of creating the rules, because if they give someone an advantage, then competition turns into the opposite of what it's supposed to be: it becomes a hidden monopoly and leads to chaos. So genuine competition is possible only when there's a developed civil society and a state governed by the rule of law. These things go together, rather like a set menu. If there is no constitutional state governed by the rule of law watching over the economy, then it will be impossible to build an economy based on the principles of competition.

And this is where we come to the most important point. There are countries like South Korea where a monopolistic private company that is under the control of a constitutional state works efficiently. There are countries like Switzerland or Norway where state corporations controlled by a democratic state work very efficiently (just look at the Swiss railway system). But there are no countries where a state or a private monopoly that is controlled by an authoritarian and corrupt state works efficiently. A combination that starts out like this nearly always ends up like Venezuela.

Corrupt and unchanging authorities (a political monopoly) together with an economic monopoly is a combination guaranteed to be a disaster.

Such a combination is malignant. Multifarious clan groups rip the very fabric of the state to shreds in trying to grab one of these monopolies for themselves. Igor Sechin came along and grabbed Rosneft. The Rotenberg brothers came along and got the Platon company to make money out of transport. And so it goes on, right down to the bottom, where you end up with situations like what happened in Kushchovskaya. These monopolies all came about thanks to the corruption of the authorities, and they can't exist without it. A whole vicious circle of corruption grows up, of 'power – monopoly – power', and this can be broken only by a revolution. This will go on forever, until an alternative model of political competition is presented that brings competition to these economic and social monopolies. And that, in turn, brings about political competition.

17

The Social Choice: A Turn to the Left or a Turn to the Right?

There are few things more deeply rooted in contemporary politics than the division between 'the left' and 'the right'. Yet at the same time it's one of the most blurred distinctions. Nowadays anyone can call themselves 'left' or 'right' as the mood takes them. The left and right agendas have become indistinguishable. The extreme right-winger, Donald Trump, came to power with a programme built on left-wing, populist stereotypes.

At one time, Putin seized the left-wing 'anti-oligarch' agenda from the Communists, then carried out a hard right-wing policy in favour of the bureaucrats and the new oligarchs. It's become extremely difficult in today's politics to determine exactly who is who.

A lot of water has flowed under the bridge since the time when it was possible to determine the left and the right depending on where people sat in the French parliament. 'Leftism' and 'rightism' were defined differently then.

Usually, those labelled left-wingers were zealous supporters of state-owned property, fanatics of big government and the regulated economy, and champions of high taxes for the 'haves' and massive preferential treatment for the 'have-nots'. At the other end of the scale, people usually called themselves right-wingers if they were supporters of the free market, adherents of small government, preferred to give out fishing rods instead of fish and were convinced that when Jesus Christ fed the five thousand he could have got by with three loaves instead of five, so as not to increase the national debt.

Sticking to my task here, I'll confine myself to a working understanding of left and right, even if it's incomplete. It seems to me that the attitude to equality lies at the basis of the division into left and right. Typical for left-wing politics is the desire to strengthen equality and eradicate inequality. In right-wing politics there is the inherent acknowledgement of inequality, especially in terms of what people own, *but in much else besides and, above all, an attempt to stimulate economic activity specifically through inequality.*

I accept that these are the extremes. Between them there are many mixed areas: we might call them 'left-rightist' or 'right-leftist'. But the heart of the matter is somewhere in here.

Neither in society as a whole nor among experts is there a united approach to the question of equality (let's not confuse this with equal rights). Therefore, there can't be a united approach to left- or right-wing politics. Rather like fashion, the attitude to inequality experiences seasonal changes. When, like now, the level of genuine inequality in the world starts to increase, the level of concern about it increases too. A whole host of studies appear that highlight the appalling economic, social and political consequences of inequality. And as a result, left-wing ideology becomes more popular.

When levelling out begins to triumph everywhere, and thus economic growth falls and the poverty that was the original reason for this levelling out becomes excessive, another wave of studies appears, no smaller than the previous one, illustrating the dangers of equality and the usefulness of inequality. Consequently, right-wing views gain more adherents.

From this we can draw the very straightforward conclusion that there is no absolute, definitive truth in either left-wing or right-wing ideologies. They are like the movements into the wind of a sailing boat. In order to sail forwards, you have to tack, now going a little to the right, now a little to the left. This in turn illustrates that the change from a course to right or left is a cyclical process, and indeed the natural thing to do. To some extent, the art of politics lies in knowing at just which point to switch from the left to the right and vice versa.

The peculiarity of the historical period we're now in is that the moment has arrived for such a change of tack. But due to the complexity of economics and politics, and the way in which they've become multidimensional, it's increasingly difficult to determine which way we need to change – from the right to the left, or from the left to the right. At times of such uncertainty, temporary leaders appear, with vague ideological profiles; people such as Trump, Boris Johnson, Matteo Salvini, and Vladimir Putin. At one moment they seem left-wing, at the next right-wing. No one can be absolutely sure in which direction their political course is heading. Quite possibly this is their aim, because they want to appeal to as broad a section of the public as possible (and so far they've succeeded in this). But they can't go on like this forever. At some point, politicians will appear on the scene with a clear programme.

Who's standing on the threshold today and knocking on the door of global politics? The left or the right? The answer to this question is not as obvious as it might seem. At first glance it looks as if Europe – and not only Europe – is on the brink of a long-expected victory for the so-called far-right forces. We have Marine Le Pen in France, the Alternativ für Deutschland (the Alternative for Germany, the AfD), the Lega Nord (Northern League) in Italy, among others. This far-right trend is so obvious that the new-found 'Russian Tsar' decided to use these forces to build a 'Holy Alliance' to defend traditional European values. But I think there's a serious question as to what extent these forces that have positioned themselves as being on the right are actually dedicated to right-wing ideas. Most of them hold a hidden left-wing agenda up their sleeve. The reason that they've had such success in the game of political poker is that the genuine left has temporarily dropped out of the race, having got lost in the mess of migration policy, thus leaving their original place open for the right.

What is it that's so confusing the traditional left and even forcing them to cower in the corner, giving up their place on the pedestal to the right, who are promoting leftist ideas? The answer lies right on the surface. The traditional left-wing programme turned out to be smeared with a migration agenda that was superimposed on top of it. This is all rooted in the split at the traditional base of left-wing ideas and the separation from the base of the 'new poor' and the 'uninvited poor'.

The 'new poor' are those who are relatively poor; that is, although their standard of living is incomparably higher than genuinely poor people in the past, they nevertheless consider themselves poor compared to the growing wealth of the 'new rich', which gives them a sense of poverty.

The 'uninvited poor' are genuinely poor people, mainly immigrants, who are temporarily and illegally employed, and who are not protected by the law. There are huge numbers of such people in the developed economies of the world.

So the problem for the left with its traditional agenda is that their social base is disappearing before their very eyes. The poor are rapidly turning into the new poor, and are ready to fight on two fronts: against both the new rich and the uninvited poor. And since (as is well known) the fiercest competition always erupts on your own doorstep, the fight against the uninvited occupies the minds of the new poor even more than the fight against the rich.

All of this was brilliantly demonstrated by the Jeremy Corbyn case in Britain. Even the Labour Party's ultra-radical social programme could not conquer the topic of Brexit in the eyes of their traditional electorate, which led to the failure of the party (along with the Conservatives) in the election for the European Parliament.

The right poured into this gap. Adopting a pseudo-leftist programme, they took advantage of the confusion of the traditional left, who were undecided on the issue of immigration, and achieved significant success. There are reasons to believe, however, that this success could be temporary. This is certainly not because the ideas of the left have some special sacred power. It's just that the left agenda is once again in demand. After a few decades dominated by the policies of the right, there's been a sharp growth in inequality and social stratification. The next long cycle will be dedicated to fighting inequality, not the other way round. This will be followed by something else, and someone will raise the banner of this just cause, whatever it may be. But here and now in the West we can most likely expect a global 'turn to the left', which I've been talking about in various formats for the past fifteen years.

This is the general background picture. So what about Russia? How does all this reflect on the country's prospects? As always, Russia is also taken up by this trend, but here it's rather more confused, because where the left and the right align there's not so much a dislike of immigrants as there is, first, a nostalgia for socialism, which is confused with the idea of a welfare state, and, second, some real remnants of socialism, which are burnt into the class nature of Russian society.

In the popular imagination, the USSR was a country in which there was no inequality. This is so – but also, not so. If you look at the absolute numbers, then they show that the difference between an ordinary worker and a member of the Politburo wasn't so great, particularly by today's standards. But in relative terms, the differences between the strata of Soviet society were enormous and constantly growing. For ideological reasons, this growth was hidden by a lack of conspicuous consumption or publicity, and wasn't apparent right up until the last moment. But when Communism died, the situation got out of hand, and Russia looked like a country with one of the highest levels of inequality. But it's wrong to say that inequality arose in the 'nineties. Because it was handled badly, the issue of inequality only came into the open in the 'nineties and destroyed the truce that then existed in society.

Russia entered the twenty-first century as a country with one of the highest inequality indices in the world (similar to the USA). The gap in earnings and the standard of living of the different strata of society became even more unacceptable in light of the long-established Soviet tradition of at least an outward appearance of equality. This meant that, at the start of the century, it was virtually impossible for right-wing ideas to be promoted in any democratic way in Russia. Against the background of the increasingly sharp stratification of society and with nostalgia for the Soviet past clearly growing, any idea that justified the further stratification of society directly or indirectly would simply have been rejected by the masses right from the start.

People were presented with a difficult choice: either accept the ideas of the right, under whose banner the post-Soviet economic reforms were carried out, including the return of a right to private property; or go for the introduction of democracy, which was the purpose of the political reforms. At that particular moment of Russia's historical development, the ideas of the right and democracy were already incompatible.

It was at that point, finding ourselves in a position where we could rethink many of the old stereotypes, and unexpectedly realizing that we were able to look at things from a different point of view, that I suggested to the reformers and the democrats – basically, all those who were ready to look to the future rather than the past, and who could see Russia as a contemporary, modernized state – to make an unambiguous choice in favour of democracy, and to change the banner. My point was that society would no longer accept the ideas of the right (even though their potential hadn't been exhausted in Russia, and the work that was worth doing under this banner was far from completed), and that this had led me to call for a 'turn to the left'.

In proposing to make this significant change of direction, I did not, however, become a supporter of Communist or left-wing ideas. I had in mind something different. I understood that the stratification of society had reached dangerous levels, which wouldn't be considered acceptable. In a country like Russia, adhering to purely libertarian views when carrying out reforms was simply utopian. The government could no longer just be a bystander, and would have to take economic and political measures to try to level out the emerging social imbalance. Eventually, this meant that we would have to part from the dream of achieving a 'small state' in Russia, and would have instead to learn how to govern and control a normal state in a normal way.

Unfortunately, many of those to whom I addressed my plea didn't listen. Indeed, for reasons beyond my control, I was unable to participate actively in this discussion, and could merely observe from the sidelines. The backbone of the forces that were resisting the creeping authoritarianism and neo-totalitarianism refused to compromise with the regime. They were brave, sometimes desperate, people, who continued the ideological and political struggle for human rights, against despotism and in favour of democratic values. These people held on to their right-wing, even libertarian, positions, speaking out for the free market, the advantages of capitalism and the joys of the small state. Maybe this was justified, but in that situation it was hardly either appropriate or practical.

The situation worsened, because, in the absence of any genuine left-leaning ideas in Russia, all that remained were fully left-wing or pseudo-left ideas. The ideological and political space was full of actors who parasitically played on the older generation's Soviet nostalgia, and pushed left-wing ideas as a tranquilizer on society. Not surprisingly, among quite a large part of the critical thinkers in the nascent civil society there developed a suspicion of the very term 'left-wing'. They began to reject everything that was associated with the left, seeing it as simply archaic Soviet thinking. As a result of this, that space was left empty.

As we all know, nature abhors a vacuum, and the ideas of the left were bought by the most unexpected client: the ruling regime. Those to whom I addressed my thoughts didn't listen to me, but in the Kremlin they understood only too well the value of left-wing ideas. Of course, I'd suggested that these ideas should be linked to a democratic agenda, but in the Kremlin they seized the programme of the left and instead used it as a means of suffocating democracy and creating post-Soviet authoritarianism. Under the cover of popular slogans about doing battle with the oligarchs, the Kremlin began to spin a false left-wing programme, pretending that it was aimed at closing the gap between the rich and the poor, promising to develop wide-ranging social programmes, and advertising their model of a welfare state. The height of this populism came in 2007–8, when they began actively to push the idea of national programmes for health care, education, culture, and so on.

At first, this undemocratic 'turn to the left' began to show very promising political possibilities. Against a background of bountiful profits from the sale of raw materials at very high prices, and giving the impression of continuing to maintain stable relations with the West (which made it possible to attract even more loans and investments), they were able to divert significant resources to the social sector, thus raising the standard of living of a reasonable part of the population to near pre-crisis levels, and in some instances even beating Soviet standards. This led to strong support in society for the regime, and also to the well-known pact with the population of 'bread in exchange for democracy', as a result of which the closed authoritarian system began to be formed.

However, Putin's social paradise didn't last long. These policies didn't lead to any kind of new equality. True, compared to the 1990s the incomes and standard of living of a significant part of the population rose significantly. But the income of the main beneficiaries of Putin's policies – the new bureaucracy and the semi-criminal businesses attached to it like glue – rose even faster, at almost astronomical speed. Social stratification not only didn't go down, but grew noticeably. A new class of oligarchs appeared, Putin's, made up of his *oprichniki*, and the incomes of the majority of the old layer of super-rich also grew. What was happening in Moscow at the national level was repeated many times over in the provinces, where the gap between social groups also widened in the same way. An amazing picture emerged: in carrying out verbally a left-wing programme, the regime actually managed to create an even greater division in society, and the growth of inequality in all areas. What's more, this was done in the most primitive, almost feudal, form.

As long as there wasn't just *a lot* of money around, but *an awful lot* of money, the regime heard no complaints about their pseudo-left agenda. Excess profits made it possible to buy off the masses painlessly, hardly affecting the rate at which those around the Kremlin were lining their pockets. But such a 'lightness of being' corrupts. Increasingly, socialist ideas became mixed in with nationalist and even militaristic ideas. And, as is well known, socialism and nationalism can often be a dangerous mix. Specifically, from the very beginning this turn towards nationalist social programmes was accompanied by the ideas outlined in Putin's Munich speech of 2007. This beginning then saw the seizure in 2008 of two regions from Georgia, South Ossetia and Abkhazia, and, as 'Putin's socialism' reached the peak of its flowering and the well-being of the post-Soviet people was at its height, in 2014 the war against

Ukraine was started. Suddenly things hit a snag. In conditions of war there was no longer enough money to keep supporting the social illusion.

What happened to Putin's welfare state when the era of hybrid wars began? In short, it drowned.

First of all, after the financial crisis of 2008 the international situation changed and the price of raw materials started to fall on its own.

Second, preparation for war and the re-establishment of a supposedly autonomous military-industrial complex (even one created just for show) is an expensive business, and, what's more, in a thoroughly corrupt state it's an inadmissible luxury even for the strongest budget.

Next, being denied long-term access to global credit markets and subjected to trade restrictions because of the imposition of sanctions is no laughing matter, no matter what they might say on Russian TV's Channel One. It seems that only the Iskander missiles might find this funny. Everyone else in Russia is crying.

Lastly, the most progressive and economically promising part of society began to leave the country en masse, taking their money with them. Each of us has but one life; and not everyone wants to spend it behind a fence with thugs. A very basic thing happened: incomes fell, but expenses grew sharply. The pie was no longer big enough to feed everyone, and the state had to choose at whose expense they could continue to 'raise the country up from its knees'.

So where should a democratically minded citizen stand on all this? Should they support the right or the left? In fact, the question itself is now wrong. As mentioned above, in the contemporary world the juxtaposition of left and right movements, or left and right ideas, is insignificant and relative at best. This is especially the case in Russia. Both left and right are now merely tactical moves, not long-term political strategies as they used to be. There is no 'left-wing Putin' or 'right-wing Trump'. Now it's all a myth and opportunistic. And, of course, the left and the right in Russia are not at all the same as they are in Europe.

What's the classic agenda of the right in the West? It's the opportunity to earn as much as possible and not share it with others, in the first place via taxes that are paid to the state. Therefore, both the state and taxes should be small. Another indicator of the right's agenda is its relationship to overconsumption. Almost everywhere in Europe this is frowned upon, and, in most cases, it is culturally and fiscally constrained. From this point of view, the Russian government is, in fact, right-wing; it has proclaimed a classic right-wing agenda by openly and bluntly embracing a single flat tax, while both the state and society encourage overconsumption beyond all measure.

We need to speak separately about overconsumption, and its link with the popular topic of anticorruption. Society puts up with whatever kind of monogrammed palaces our officials of the state build. Russia isn't the birthplace of elephants, but it is the birthplace of special fur coat storage vaults. And there has to be a surfeit of everything: on an Arabian scale, of African quality, and in an ostentatious Asian style. And all of it accompanied by a pretension to being another Versailles! There are few countries on this planet that display such demonstrative overconsumption. And it doesn't matter whether you've done this with stolen money or your own.

What's important here is that in any normal society this would be considered vulgar. But in Russia, it's acceptable. Our society – in contrast to the West – reacts perfectly calmly both to a flat tax rate and to barbaric overconsumption. People might not like it, but there's no class hatred. What's more, many people will react far more harshly to the slightest privilege displayed by a neighbour than they will to the luxury of an unknown wealthy person. A neighbour's front door reinforced with iron will anger them more than the forged metal fence around Igor Sechin's dacha. Let me explain.

The answer is not obvious. It's more thanks to history and philosophy than to politics. When it comes to consumption, Russia retains a rudimentary class structure and, accordingly, a scale of social aspirations. Therefore, Russians' demands of the authorities when it comes to social policy are still restricted as a function of class.

People don't ask for much; but they'll never give up the little they have. They hold tightly to the status quo and their modest social benefits, and do not wish to lose them, even when these benefits are merely of a symbolically practical significance. The privileges of the upper layers of society bother people much less than many think they do.

The story about pension reform is completely irrational only at first glance. People were very upset by the raising of the pensionable age, even though, in a practical sense, this move by the government would affect most of them only in the distant future, if at all. But this was less of a practical issue than something that upset the balance: although these were future privileges being taken away, they were nonetheless psychologically important ones for the lower levels of society.

In contrast to the West, most Russians recognize class boundaries, and don't try to break them (an individual might jump over them, that's fine; just don't break them). But this notwithstanding, they demand that the quality of life within those class boundaries be maintained and even improved. And if there's any small lowering of standards, however insignificant it might seem in the grand scheme of things, they will react with howls of protest. The question as to whether it's possible to break these class barriers in the near future, let alone whether it needs to be done at all, remains an open one. This question is certainly not at the forefront of people's minds, because for it to be so there would have to be a genuine revolution in their consciousness.

The class nature of Russian society hinders the development of a genuine left-wing programme in the country. Apart from the nationalization of the economy, what's a typical left-wing agenda in Europe? It means a progressive rate of income tax. But there can't even be any discussion of this in Russia. People simply don't understand how making things worse for one level of society can improve the situation for their own level. They just don't see any connection. The 13 per cent tax rate in Russia is quite simply not a subject for serious discussion. This is why, in Russia, there's no structured left-wing agenda. It would have to be created, bearing in mind the specifics of the class system.

A properly built social policy is a powerful lever for overturning the pyramid of power. Why is this so important? Putin isn't a mixed politician; he's a radical right-winger. The left is just a false cloak that he dons. As he imitates the technologies of fascist-type leaders, rather like Solaris he changes his mask to suit the situation. Since 2003 he's been covering up his course with left-wing slogans. But, like everything else in his regime, the left-wing programme he has declared is just for show. There's actually nothing new in this. Just as there's no genuine self-governance and no genuine federalism, Putin has no genuine left agenda. He will, though, continue to use the left-wing mask in the future as the situation demands, as his regime becomes ever more decrepit.

Given all this, the situation will only continue to go downhill. Matters will go from bad to worse, since, in the global division of labour, there's no place for Russia in the industrial production sphere. Conveyor belts aren't our thing; and, in any case, this place is already taken. Only highly skilled labour could save us, but unfortunately we're lowering the prestige of education and cutting off the funding for it. The class nature of society keeps growing. Our children don't see the value of higher education, and consequently they'll have nowhere to go when they grow up. It's programmed mass impoverishment.

It's quite possible that there's a subconscious political element here: it's easier to manage a poor society. Poor people's expectations are lower.

In this way, too, Putin is ensuring that the class system will remain for decades to come. The model being laid down means that the majority of the population will be unable to move up because of a lack of qualifications. You can't evolve out of such a system. You can only smash it.

The regime can be and has to be caught out on this. The democratic movement should put forward a genuine left-wing tactical programme in opposition to the regime's leftist show. Not an abstract European programme (that wouldn't work in Russia), but one designed for the reality of the Russian class system. What does a tactical left-wing programme for contemporary Russian conditions look like? It's nothing supernatural. It's a combination of two things. A consistent battle against overconsumption and strict guarantees that niche measures of social support for the broad mass of the population will be at least maintained at current levels, and where possible expanded.

It seems that it's impossible to fight against overconsumption in Russia, because there's no clearly expressed demand for this from society, despite the opposition's clear anticorruption campaign. People feel indignation, but this simply borders on philistine curiosity and doesn't develop into energy for political action. As a result, everything disappears into the sand.

There is, though, one small but significant detail. People are ready to accept overconsumption by the fathers, but they're not prepared to recognize the children's rights to it. The legitimacy of inheriting large fortunes in Russia, be they in the families of oligarchs or the dynasties of government officials, remains an open question. Tolerating the class system doesn't pass on to the next generation. So there's a window of opportunity for an evolutionary solution to this problem, through the introduction of confiscatory inheritance tax rates for excessively large fortunes.

As for social guarantees for wide swathes of the population, Russia is doomed to remain a welfare state where the vestiges of Soviet socialism will be around for a long time. Experiments that the regime gets sucked into like a whirlpool from time to time, such as monetizing benefits or raising the pensionable age, are untenable politically in Russia.

The democratic movement will gain mass support only if it is able to take a firm and unequivocal position on this question. All financial and fiscal questions have to be solved by increasing the pace of growth of the economy, reducing the costs that corruption imposes on society, and introducing an inheritance tax – and not through some sacred inviolable stockpile of Soviet-era benefits.

To sum up, at the current time the tactical left-wing agenda of the democratic movement could be presented in two parts. On the one hand, phasing out overconsumption through a confiscatory inheritance tax on excessively large fortunes. And, on the other, guaranteeing to maintain (and even planning to gradually increase) basic social benefits, primarily in health care, education and social security.

Over recent years, the falseness of the regime's social policy has been exposed for all to see. The left-wing programme has become nothing but ritualistic bare-minimum superficial fluff. While continuing occasionally to pay lip service to its 'national projects', in reality the government has waged a full-scale war on its own population in the name of an 'optimization' of social spending. Almost a third of educational and medical establishments have gone under the knife. They've even killed the sacred cow of the socialist past: the low pensionable age. And the federal multiple-child benefit has all but faded to nothing because of the devaluation of the rouble, becoming just another benefit that doesn't really have any impact on people's lives, and so on.

But another sacred cow has survived: the windfall profits of the ruling clan, which have successfully passed through all the de-offshorization, the capital increasing both when the funds were taken out of the country and when they were brought back in. The height of cynicism was the massive buyout by the state of illiquid assets at inflated prices from entrepreneurs who already feed out of the hands of the state, and granting compensation from the federal budget to those affected by sanctions.

This latter looks particularly disgusting against the background of 'the parmesan war': the counter-sanctions that 'bombed Voronezh', by removing from the middle class their access to quality food products. In this way, and in conditions of a crisis and an undeclared war against the West, the regime has effectively begun implementing a typical right-wing policy agenda: optimization for the benefit of the rich at the expense of the poor. It was less a question of 'Crimea is ours' than 'Crimea has been taken at our expense'.

If these tendencies continue (and there's no reason to suppose that they'll change radically) then the subject of a 'turn to the left' will become as relevant as it was fifteen years ago. Social division will grow at triple the pace, now not only because of the new rich, but also because of the recently created new poor, whose well-being has fallen dramatically as a result of crisis optimization brought about by the undeclared war. And the subjects of poverty, social inequality and the unjust distribution of resource rent will return to the top of the political agenda. But the regime that's sunk into a war to try to gather in the slivers of empire will no longer have the ability to take hold of this agenda.

We can assume that the resistance movement will face the same dilemma as it did at the start of the century: should we make a 'turn to the left' and come to power democratically, or should we choose the ideas of the right and face yet more political isolation?

In conditions of rapidly increasing inequality, when left-wing ideas are gaining ever more adherents in society, reckoning on coming to power by democratic means on the back of a right-wing and even an ultra-right-wing programme, which is frequently libertarian, and which acclaims the joys of the 'small state' and the potential of the free market – this is all an absurd utopia. Acting in this way, that part of civil society that's most ready to take on the fight risks disappearing forever from the political stage, and passing not just into the stalls but to the upper circle. And the stage will be taken over by comedians and opportunists.

Once again, we are facing the same conditions today as we were when I wrote 'A Turn to the Left'. For the opposition it would be an inexcusable luxury to pass up this chance to return to the world of live politics, instead of playing games on Facebook.

If a democratic coalition with a left-wing agenda is unable to come together, then the chances of there being a peaceful transition of power by democratic means are not great. The regime will continue to hang by a thread until that thread is cut by a revolution from below, and on the wave of that revolution new Bolsheviks will come to power. If this is the case, there's a real risk that Russian history will find itself running yet another penalty lap, and, as a result, Russia will become irrelevant in world history – only this time forever.

18

The Intellectual Choice: Freedom of Speech or Glasnost on a Reservation?

Whenever the conversation turns to discussing the political regime in Russia, those who try somehow to classify it inevitably end up experiencing cognitive dissonance. On the one hand, the regime undoubtedly appears to be authoritarian, repressive and even totalitarian. Those in power are irremovable, the opposition has no chance whatsoever of winning through elections that are merely a formality, and any citizen can fall foul of arbitrary police thuggery at any moment, even if they're not involved in politics in any way, and all the more so if they are involved in politics.

It used to be possible to write about all this relatively directly and openly online, and even on certain mass media channels that had reasonably open access. The authorities could be criticized, you could carry out independent investigations, dig up the dirt on senior government officials, and so on. And basically, people got away with it, although there were individual cases involving certain prominent journalists who lost their lives. But such things happen in other countries, too; in recent years, for example, this has occurred in Slovakia, Bulgaria and Malta.

It should be noted that, until recently, you could express your opinion in Putin's Russia more easily than you ever could in the USSR, even in the most liberal times. Ekho Moskvy radio, the *Novaya Gazeta* newspaper, TV Rain [*Dozhd*], a comparatively open internet and much, much more would have been simply unimaginable in the Soviet Union. You could have been locked up for a long time even for dreaming about such a thing. This is why many people have spoken and written about Russia as if it were a reasonably free country – or at least a country where there was freedom of speech. Was this justified?

The problem is that freedom of speech in the literal meaning of the words is the highest legal and constitutional principle that a state must adhere to. This freedom is guaranteed by the full force of civil society, and of the political state of which it is a part. But there is no such freedom in modern Russia. In its place there is a space, the boundaries of which are strictly defined by the state, with whose permission, and under whose watchful gaze, an exotic beast named 'Glasnost' is permitted to dwell. This lonely old animal lives in a special reservation allotted to it on the edge of a police state, and is there for the amusement of gawking Muscovites and visiting tourists.

Life on the reservation depends entirely on the will of the state: it could shut it down entirely at any moment, but for some unknown reason of its own it hasn't done this. Apparently, the harm that would come from closing the reservation (with the fuss that this would cause, the need to distract the gawkers with something else, and so on) for now is considered greater than the harm this illusory openness might bring to the regime. The situation didn't just happen in an instant, but built up historically under the influence of a multitude of factors that were varied and at times contradictory. In order to understand how to get out of this situation and, more importantly, where to go after that, it's essential to give a brief description of how it evolved.

In the Soviet Union, society was just about as closed as it could be in a practical sense. This closed nature of society gave unique opportunities to state propaganda, which helped the regime to control people's consciousness, and thus the behaviour of the majority. Herein lies one of the main differences between a totalitarian regime and an authoritarian one. The former relies not only on police repression, but also on the active programming of people's consciousness and their behaviour with the help of an all-powerful propaganda machine. The present regime doesn't have anything like this, and I don't think it will ever succeed in creating it.

From the mid-fifties, when the era of the Great Terror had passed, the main responsibility for maintaining the stability of the Soviet system was laid on the state's propaganda machine. The repressive structures assisted in this, by weeding out those who, for one reason or another, were immune to the propaganda. But such people were relatively few, and so the state's repressive machinery didn't have to be kept permanently active. It was working behind the scenes, only occasionally removing those who thought differently. All the main dirty work was done by the Party wordsmiths.

The state's propaganda machine was unprecedented in its power and operated at every level of society. Because of this, any true information about what was happening in the country and in the world was kept hidden from the people. This naturally came to define the principal front line of the struggle against the regime both inside the USSR and from outside. What annoyed the vast majority of people most in the final years of Soviet power wasn't the organs of repression, it wasn't the militia [as the police were called in Soviet times – Tr.] or the KGB, with whom the overwhelming majority of the population had no direct contact; rather, it was the Party propagandists, who'd been telling the nation tales that simply didn't fit in with their own everyday experiences.

We didn't have to wait long to see the logical conclusion to such a situation. When Mikhail Gorbachev came to power, the main demand coming from those both at the top and at the bottom of society was to know the truth. In answer to this political demand, voiced loudly and clearly, the leadership under Gorbachev came up with the slogan of 'glasnost', or 'openness'. Of course, glasnost was a purely Soviet euphemism, reflecting a vague and mythologized view on the part of the Soviet party elite about such interrelated liberal values as freedom of speech, freedom of the press, openness, and so on. It was indeed an extremely inconsistent, limited and internally contradictory ideological concept. But at the same time, it's important to understand that it was the most fundamental, the very first, and thus the most stringent paradigm of perestroika. It was the backbone on which everything else was then hung.

Psychologically, glasnost was seen from the outset as the principal achievement of Gorbachev's revolution, and that opinion remains to this day. It was seen as a focused response to Soviet totalitarianism, as witnessed by the last generations of the Soviet period. That was why, when the regime began its attack on democracy, and all the achievements of the revolution brought about by Gorbachev and Boris Yeltsin were thrown out, glasnost became the last unsinkable bastion of Communist liberalism.

For many people, this has created the illusion that some sort of freedom of speech has survived in Russia. In reality, the situation has been much more complicated. Even before the war began there was no freedom of speech in Russia. But the authoritarian, and to some extent even neo-totalitarian, regime partially learnt to coexist with the remnants of Gorbachev's glasnost, which even brought it some benefits.

Of course, the start of the war and the regime's switch to a state of totalitarian mobilization could not but affect this area of life. All the influential independent and semi-independent media, journalists and bloggers came under unprecedented pressure, as a result of which they had either to stop working, or leave the country, or go over to the service of the regime.

However, this is the final stage of the development of a dictatorship. We have to understand how to keep such an evolution from taking place.

In order to correctly build a strategy to democratize Russian society in the future, it's essential that we understand the secret of the strange and sometimes unnatural coexistence of the two mutually exclusive foundations of the life of society: the truth and the lie.

The basis of this phenomenon is the regime's ability to hold control of the commanding heights of information. It all began when the basic channels of information became concentrated in the hands of the state and the people and structures affiliated with it. The significant moment in this process was the destruction of the old NTV television channel, and the re-establishment of full control over Channel One by the presidential administration. At this point, Channel One became a public broadcasting organization in name only. Today, the information market in Russia is one of the biggest monopolies.

What's more, the state directly or indirectly controls not only the pro-government media, but even the bulk of the media that is considered to be on the side of the opposition.

The state's expansion in this area wasn't just restricted to the classic media. The growth of the internet saw the state's agents move in there, too. A vital line was crossed here when they acquired control of the largest social network in Russia, VKontakte (VK). Along with this, massive budgetary funds are pumped into various internet projects through numerous intermediary contractors. Despite the widespread view that the Russian part of the internet opposes the regime, the state is actually the dominant player here, too.

What's even more important, though, are not the quantitative indicators but the qualitative ones. It's not just which part of the information sphere belongs to the state that really matters, it's also how it is used. As a result of the endless efforts the Kremlin has put in over many years, it has created what might be called a dominating flow of information. Its very aggressive method of all-out dissemination of information is like a permanent information war.

This dominating information flow is generated from the Kremlin, and its transmission belt is the huge network of Kremlin agents who run specific information resources, on several levels at once. This is an extremely complicated system, which includes a many-branched and decentralized network of think-tanks – analytical factories churning out a flow of ideas. It has its own numerous and mostly outsourced production facilities, its own 'stars' and its own 'cannon fodder'. This system is much more finely tuned and sophisticated than the repressive security bloc, which is not surprising; until recently, it played a key role in stabilizing the regime.

It was this powerful state-controlled information flow that allowed the regime to keep a weak and limited alternative information stream nearby on the reservation, the noise of which was almost inaudible to the masses, since it was drowned out by the roar of the main flow. Even while allowing glasnost to frolic around in the information sandpit, the regime kept strict control over the doses of information it permitted in the 'marketplace', gauging how much was allowed as if it were using a chemist's scales. This means that it has to have indirect control over the opposition media, and this control has been steadily increasing. Any attempt to leave the confines of the 'sandpit' has led to scandals, and to the opposition being roughly forced back into line.

But any complex system is quite fragile. What works on small-scale protests starts to shudder and crash on large ones. With ever-increasing political loads on the system, it becomes more and more difficult to generate the flow they need. What's more, the interference created by alternative information currents that are confined to the reservation is becoming more noticeable and more dangerous for the system. As a result, the system has had to be amended and the dominating flow turned into an all-out flow. This signified the end of the era of truncated, postmodern glasnost and a return to the full and simple Soviet model.

By its very nature, glasnost is very vulnerable. It's a secondary device and is derived from the authorities themselves. Starting in 1999 – that is, throughout the whole period of post-Communist reaction – we've been witnessing the regime's attack on glasnost as it limits the space available to it, both directly and indirectly. And all the while, there was a genuine threat of a complete clampdown on glasnost, and when the regime decided to carry this out, no one and nothing could stop it. But at the same time, this results in unpleasant and irreversible consequences not only for society, but also for the regime itself. It will not so much slow it down as hasten its end.

Well, you might say, to hell with them, let them tighten the screws as much as they want then! But the important thing is not so much when the regime will collapse as what will take its place. This is why, of course, the defence of any kind of glasnost has a huge significance for the democratic movement.

No matter how insubstantial the truth that is shut up on a reservation may be, it's better than a lie that's wandering around freely. We must fight for every word of truth; we must resist any attempt by the regime to get rid of glasnost once and for all; we have to do all we possibly can to help journalists and publications that heroically continue to stand up to totalitarianism, even if now most of them are doing this from abroad. But this shouldn't be our main strategic goal. We shouldn't be aiming to fully restore glasnost, but to create rock-solid constitutional guarantees of freedom of speech.

We need a qualitative leap forward in our policy of openness. I must emphasize that simply turning back the clock to the time of Vladimir Yakovlev's *Kommersant* newspaper or Igor Malashenko's NTV television channel is no longer enough. What suited the young, post-Soviet society wouldn't suit a society that has gained great and varied experience in fighting for democracy. Even if we were to ignore what Putin has sliced off it, Gorbachev's version of glasnost is no longer the ideal that we should be striving for.

We have to go further, to a fully free and open information market, regulated by very precise laws. Only such a market, where there is genuine competition, can guarantee that the right to freedom of speech will be ensured.

Of course, a free market environment would solve some problems and at the same time create new ones, so society is facing no small number of complicated questions to which it must find the answers. But this doesn't change my choice of the strategic direction we must move in: competition and the market should provide society with genuine openness.

It stands to reason that, in a sense, only a properly functioning democratic political system can provide freedom of speech. This means there would have to be genuine separation of powers, a properly functioning justice system, and so on, and, most importantly, society's readiness to protect this freedom using armed force if necessary. If freedom of speech is political currency, then it has to be guarded by the whole democratic infrastructure of society. But alongside all these general guarantees, there are specific measures, including institutional ones, without which there can be no freedom of speech.

Among these specific measures there are economic and political ones. Each of these helps to achieve the single main aim: not only to prevent the state from restricting freedom of speech, but also to remove the possibility that it could begin dominating the flow of information yet again, thanks to which it is able to manipulate the population with the help of lies, notwithstanding the continuing existence of the islands of free speech built into the system. The democratic movement must learn its lesson from the experience of post-Communist neo-totalitarianism to ensure that this mistake is not repeated.

I'll start with the economic measures.

However paradoxical this may seem, the main problem for the Russian press is not censorship, but poverty. The main challenges in the battle for freedom in recent decades were not fought on the political front, as many think, but on the economic front. There has never been a truly economically independent media in post-Communist Russia. Up until the default of 1998, the media retained some freedom to manoeuvre – they had freedom of choice as to who to depend on, which sources of funding they could trust, and therein lay a certain independence. From then on, the state started the process of taking over the media entirely, and between 2006 and 2008, or thereabouts, it became the media's sole patron, directly or indirectly. It was at that point that the fiercest and most frightening blows were rained down on the freedom of the press and, consequently, on freedom of speech, and the media was never able to recover from this.

Furthermore, rather than openly and systematically supporting independent media and helping them out of difficulty, the government made use of the situation and carried out a large-scale, indirect nationalization of these outlets by replacing their owners with state-sanctioned personnel – often by way of police raids and by using criminal indictments to exert pressure. The 'catch' was divided up between various state-owned companies and financial and industrial groups affiliated with the regime. In time, the state (as the owner or sponsor) took indirect control over all the more or less significant information resources. The picture looks even more depressing when you turn from the giants of the media market to the provincial press, which was already in a dire state.

At first sight, an ideal solution to the problem might appear to be to create normal market conditions for the media, both the traditional and online media, where the state would take on only the role of impartial arbiter and regulator. But unfortunately, global practice shows that nowadays this doesn't work.

Increasingly the media is either a subsidized ancillary business, or else it exists on sponsorship funds, made on the basis of a variety of motives, including political ones.

Very few countries get by without having their media subsidized by the state; but it'll be a long time before Russia can be counted in their number. Therefore, it's important for us to see exactly how subsidizing the media from budgetary funds is carried out today and, conversely, exactly how management of mass media subsidized from budgetary funds ought to be organized. By answering these two questions in sequence, we will largely solve the problem of neutralizing the totalitarian ambitions of the state to form the dominating information flow described above.

If support for the media from the national budget is necessary and unavoidable, then we must ensure that this is transparent, and that neither individual government officials nor their fraternity as a whole benefit from these subsidies. Or, to put it more simply, that they are unable to demand a lot of small services for every 'vitamin fed (to the press)'. Everything the state does in the field of information must be done in the interests of society and under society's control, and not in the interests of the bureaucracy or controlled by the bureaucrats.

Budget funds that are dedicated to support the media must be above board, politically neutral and allocated on a competitive basis with the participation of the public. Any secret funding of media projects by the state (such as the infamous 'troll factories') must be forbidden by law, and we have to put an end to the era of spending on 'special journalism' funded by the state.

If we manage to stabilize the information market and create the conditions for the rise of a variety of free media sources that can exist either on their own resources (in other words, to be independent financially), or to have government support that's transparent and controlled by society, then we can focus on the second side of the problem: ensuring political guarantees of the independence of the media. After all, in addition to having made a slave of the media, the state has also directly invaded the information space, actively abusing its position and its resources, in this case less its economic ones than its administrative ones.

If we think about it, we have a limited number of tools at our disposal to do battle against state propaganda without limiting freedom of speech in Russia. In reality, the state plays a dual role in the media market: as a regulator that sets the rules of the game, and as a player itself. What we want from the state as a regulator is obvious: ensuring a fair competitive environment and guaranteeing freedom of speech for everyone. But what do we want from the state as a player? This is a rather more difficult one to answer. As the founder of various elements of the media, the state automatically has a great opportunity to influence their policies. But the state is a particular type of owner. In theory, we are the owners, because the state is spending not its own money, but every citizen's money. So what should happen?

Countries with a developed democratic system found the answer to this a long time ago. Information resources that have been created by the state or with the state's help are entrusted to the management of representatives of civil society. Trusts or public boards are in charge of state television and other information sources affiliated with the state. These are directly made up of representatives of civil society. By law, the state cannot influence their membership, and in practice such a possibility is restricted in all kinds of ways. The procedure for creating these bodies is carried out as transparently as possible, which ensures that their composition is independent of the authorities and respected by society. Any violations, conspiracy or pressure being applied is considered a criminal act. The activities of these institutions are regulated by special statutes (rules), which exclude the possibility of legally turning these resources into tools for manipulating public opinion in the interests of certain groups or individuals.

And the last point – last, that is, in order, but not in terms of its significance. Freedom of speech and openness were, and remain, the most important dimension of democracy: they are the cloth that binds society together. Protecting them from attack by any kind of watchdog, whoever that might be, is the most important task of the democratic movement. But freedom of speech can also be subtly used by those whose goal is the destruction of all freedom. It's very tempting not to allow them this freedom.

The subtlety of freedom of speech lies in the fact that, in this battle, it's easier than anywhere else to throw the baby out with the bathwater. It's possible to organize such a fight against state propaganda or some other evil in a way that nobody would think it was too little, and, instead of appalling propaganda, you would see even more appalling counter-propaganda. However repugnant it may seem, we have to acknowledge that any word has the right to be free. We have to be careful with any attempt to limit what can and what cannot be said, written, shown or broadcast. If you want to ban any single word at all, it could soon turn out, to your great surprise, that you've forbidden the use of a whole dictionary.

My personal position on this is that, if there's any doubt at all, then, rather like the principle that the law is on the side of the accused, we should come down in favour of freedom of speech. It's better that someone be allowed to say something disgusting than that someone be denied the opportunity to learn something important and essential. The priority that freedom should come before any restrictive measures is the main principle that should be adhered to so as not to stray from the course.

I remain convinced that, for example, the incredibly boring *Mein Kampf,* full as it is of hatred for mankind, and the forged *Protocols of the Elders of Zion,* just like the secret protocol added to the pact between Hitler and Stalin, should be available to anyone who's interested in reading them, and should not become some sort of secret knowledge.

It can be very difficult to carry this out in practice, even psychologically. But we have to learn and, rather than simply banning it, find alternative methods of suppressing the appearance of extremism in all its manifestations.

We have to learn to live in a world where we constantly exist alongside things that we find unacceptable. It is only in such a world that life is genuinely stable and comfortable.

19

The Constitutional Choice:
A Parliamentary Republic or a
Presidential Republic?

Arguments about whether there should be a presidential
or a parliamentary republic in Russia flare up and die
down repeatedly in the country's political discussions.
From a purely utilitarian point of view, this doesn't seem all
that urgent a topic, and rather reminds one of dividing up
the skin of a bear that isn't yet dead. A lot of people say: 'Let's
first work out the democratic content that we can dress up in
an acceptable political format, then we'll talk.' That's all well
and good, but there's one small problem: in Russia, political
content and format have become so completely intertwined
that if we don't get rid of the political format that we already
have, we won't be able to replace it with any content other than
what we have today.

So the question of how Russia's political format will look in
the future is neither speculative nor premature. The answer
to this is a kind of political litmus test, illustrating a serious
intention to break the Russian tradition of autocracy and a
readiness to carry this through to the end, and not simply
swap one type of autocracy for another, and even less, one tsar
for another. This is not a question of constitutional structure,
but of political philosophy, and thus it is a deeply ideological

question. Perhaps this is why it has to be settled first, before anything else.

Indeed, the constitutional and legal significance of the political format in Russia has been somewhat exaggerated. In all seriousness, you can't simply argue that a parliamentary republic is more democratic than a presidential one, or vice versa. Across the world, experience shows that in both presidential and parliamentary models an acceptable format can be created for free representation of the people with a built-in and effective separation of powers. At the same time, any political format can be cut down to fit any authoritarian or even totalitarian system. It's worth reminding ourselves that, formally, the USSR was a parliamentary republic. It's more important to integrate all executive power, including the president, into a system of separation and balance of power. So what's the issue here?

The issue is Russia's specific situation – the peculiarities of its political history, culture and traditions. People frequently describe today's Russia as a presidential republic. That is, to say the least, a massive exaggeration. Not only is Russia not presidential (despite its having a president), but in the exact meaning of the term it's not even a republic. Over the past hundred years, no ruler of the Russian state has come to power through free and fair and truly democratic elections. (Even Boris Yeltsin's victory in June 1991 was achieved thanks to regional elections within the Soviet empire.)

The history of twentieth-century Russia is rather like the history of Rome in the era of the 'soldier emperors' – in most cases, the irremovable dictators either ruled the country until their death, or were overthrown by a coup. Sometimes these came together. In the same way, autocracy was, and is to this day, the only natural political format for Russia. To be more precise, it's the format and the content all at the same time. And, as the first 'red tsar', Lenin, wrote, this is 'objective reality which is given to man by his sensations'. How we react to this reality is the main question for the future of Russia and the main political watershed.

The question is this: are we prepared ruthlessly to break this long-established Russian tradition of autocracy, or, despite all the democratic slogans do we, in the depths of our souls, wish still to keep searching for a 'good tsar' who will grant Russia freedom? If we choose a presidential model, then there is far more likelihood in the future that the inborn autocratic instincts will rise to the surface of Russia's political culture once again and give those in power much greater scope to move away from democratic methods than would a parliamentary model.

This is the main – indeed, the single – reason why I consider that a parliamentary republic is the preferred option for the Russia of my dreams. We have messed around too much by experimenting with personalized models of power, which is why today we need to boldly cut right to the bone before the rot sets in again. However many times we've played with the Lego bricks of the Russian political system, we've always ended up with the same result. It's like the old joke about the worker who steals all sorts of spare parts from the factory for purely personal use, only to find that, when he gets them home and starts putting them together, he always ends up with a Kalashnikov rifle. Similarly, however many presidents of Russia you try to put together from various constitutional bits and pieces, you'll always end up with a tsar.

Even though a presidential republic is generally considered to be the opposite of a parliamentary republic, given the very many in-between, mixed formats that you can find, understanding the subtle differences between them is not so easy. The key question ultimately is the depth of the separation of powers and the exact way in which this is laid out. There's an extra dimension that provides for the separation of powers in a parliamentary republic: namely, the further division of power within the executive branch of government into the head of state and the head of the executive.

So in a parliamentary republic, we have this extra dimension of democracy. And the division of the executive can be very varied. The head of state might be a completely nominal figure (such as the British king, as in other modern constitutional monarchies); or they might play a specific political role as an arbiter (like in modern Italy); or they might carry out an important and even decisive role in power (as in France, which is a very specific type of presidential-parliamentary republic). There are no general rules or set standards in this issue.

The choice of which specific type of parliamentary republic to create is the key question when designing a future constitutional structure. To a large extent, forming an efficient model demonstrates great skill in constitutional creativity. All the successful working models of democracy have come about as a result of a creative instinct and a deep understanding of the peculiarities of a national culture.

The reality is that societies show much more clearly defined individuality than do individuals themselves. Nevertheless, there are certain principles that can be used in any circumstances to create models that work.

One of the basic principles for building a parliamentary republic is the relationship between parliament and the government. Whatever different types of parliamentary republic there might be, one factor is a constant: the head of the government and all members of that government are beholden to parliament, which appoints them and holds them to account – and can even vote them out.

Why is this important in Russia specifically? Because parliament's 'share price' will immediately rise on the political market. The same shares that until today have been classified as worthless on the Russian institutional exchange. They were bought up only by 'bears', playing for a fall. If parliament becomes the only body that can appoint and dismiss the government, then the hour of the 'bull' will come to Russia. And at that point, not only will parliament's shares rise in value, but so too will all those of the democratic cluster linked to it.

If parliament occupies the central institutional place in Russia's political system, then the value of a member's seat will also rise, leading to the same across the whole electoral procedure.

This would also mean that holding elections for candidates based solely on their personal appeal, as usually happens with Russia's presidential election, will become much more difficult. Along with this, the value of regional representation in both houses will also rise sharply, because how well these representatives can satisfy the daily needs of the local population will directly depend on their quantity and quality. In other words, the system of federal relations will have true significance, unlike the current situation in which it is nothing more than decorative in the strictly centralized, unitary state. In its turn, this will pull the compensatory development of local self-governance along with it, with the aim of preventing Russia from returning to a system of feudalism with the re-emergence of individual principalities.

So the switch to a parliamentary republic is the key element that carries with it the whole chain of democratic events.

Naturally, the change to a system of parliamentary democracy from autocracy and the strongly centralized personal system of government that's existed in Russia for centuries will be a political shock.

But it's an unavoidable and essential shock. The move to a parliamentary republic is the only possible way of rebooting the political system in Russia, and this is why – and for no other reason – it is clearly superior to a presidential republic.

'That's all well and good', the opponents of a parliamentary republic usually reply, 'but do we have the right to carry out such experiments in Russia? It's a massive country with a very specific way of life, and people are used to the idea that power is highly personalized. People won't understand or appreciate your well-intentioned plans; they will not be able to take advantage of the benefits of this parliamentary democracy, nor would they want to, and the whole thing will quickly collapse into anarchy and chaos. Added to this, Russia is still an empire, a huge melting pot, in which representatives of the most varied nationalities and confessions are mixed together, and they've never been citizens of a nation-state. If you take out the figure of the ruler who's the very personification of power (whatever their title), the country will break into pieces!'

How do we answer that one? These are not risks that have been simply dreamt up. They really do exist. The problem is that they don't go away when we switch from one personalized regime to another. If we don't alter the way Russian statehood develops, then every subsequent regime, however much it promises, will in a few years or even months inevitably become an autocracy. And each new autocracy will be worse than the previous one; there can be no doubt about that. And in the end what happens is exactly what the opponents of parliamentary democracy are afraid of: the country will fall apart. But by then there'll be no hope of saving it and it'll be forever. At least a parliamentary republic would give us a fighting chance.

All this comes down not so much to a practical political choice as to an ideological one. Do you think that an attempt to break the personalized model of governance in Russia creates unacceptable risks? Well, you have every right to think that.

But then a question arises. What are your essential disagreements with the pro-government forces that hold similar positions? Of course, in order to save Russia, they propose preserving 'caveman absolutism', while you, in turn, hope to rule for a long time with the help of 'enlightened absolutism'. But 500 years of Russian absolutism have taught us that the grey-suited pen-pushers always end up giving way to the black-shirted fascists.

The personalized model is like a political drug for Russia. No one denies that the country became addicted to it a long time ago, way before Putin came along. Coming off such a powerful drug could cause painful withdrawal symptoms in society; and it's not impossible that the process could even lead to life-threatening situations. But does this mean that we should therefore simply accept this political dependency and not try to turn away from the needle of autocracy?

Paradoxically, in the very near future we may witness those in power undertaking a simulated constitutional reform in pursuit of their own narrow self-serving political interests. One of its most important features will be a transition from a presidential republic to a parliamentary one.

This won't necessarily happen just like that, but one of the scenarios being discussed for getting around the constitutional snag that prevents Putin from being president for life after 2024 is for him to be made prime minister for life, with all power transferred to him.

Clearly such an edifice isn't going to be an actual parliamentary republic. It will just be replaced by a different veneer covering up the hideousness of an absolutist regime. This naturally raises the question: how should the democratic movement react to this pastiche of a parliamentary democracy?

The first instinctive response, of course, is rejection. Both because such a model discredits the very idea and is just a way of perpetuating the regime, and also because it is the Kremlin that is proposing it. It's like what the essayist Joseph Brodsky once said: 'If Yevtushenko is against collective farms, then I'm in favour.' But actually, whatever may have motivated the authorities to take this decision, it is still a step in the right direction.

We need to use it as a paradigm, and demand that the purely decorative parliamentary republic be made into a real one – and the irremovable prime minister into one who can be replaced after free and fair elections to a new parliament.

The paragraphs above were written long before Tereshkova's amendment was added to the Constitution [to remove presidential term limits – Ed.]. I admit that I wrongly assumed that there would be a rather higher intellectual level among the people (or person) examining the options for such a change; but I'm generally inclined to overestimate the talents of my opponents.

The authorities chose to go down the most primitive, direct and blunt route.

Rather than reforming the Constitution, we saw its destruction, so that Putin could continue in the post of president. The result of this has been war, which has sparked the discussion again, and with renewed vigour. Russia has two models of sustainable development: the static equilibrium model (autocracy), and the dynamic balance model (the federal one). Of course, Russia is under no obligation to develop. The alternative to sustainable development is stagnation and disintegration. However, I believe that the stagnation and disintegration of Russia, which, understandably, those who are fighting against Russian aggression today might wish for, could cause a drastic imbalance in the system of international relations, and create in the heart of Eurasia a group of aggressive and poorly run (even out of control) bankrupt states armed with nuclear weapons. The genuine and desired choice facing responsible players on the international stage is not one between the disintegration of Russia or its continued existence, but one between the autocratic (static) and federal parliamentary (dynamic) models of its sustainable development.

Yet another version of autocracy seems to be the simplest solution for many, including opponents of the Putin regime; but in reality this is a very unreliable option. A regime that is static and stable thanks to strict centralization and where the authorities have unlimited power will, sooner or later, lead to trouble in society. Such a system will be able to extinguish this only by diverting this excess energy onto the outside world. Even without this, war is a fundamental component of autocracy, upon which everything else is constructed. And autocratic regimes, including the Bolshevik one, are unstable in the long term (their apparent stability is only relative). They are based on the constant search for a consensus among the elite through democratic centralism. This has a significant vulnerability: as the number of participants in the process increases, the number of connections between them increases exponentially. And the single point – the head of the system – who should take the final decisions becomes no longer capable of taking into account all these various interconnections. As a way of solving this problem, the centre turns to unification – totalitarianism – which once again sets in motion the same complex of historical problems.

In any mid-term perspective, Russia's system of autocracy has a clearly defined militaristic profile. This is almost completely independent of the ideology it starts out with or the personality of the national leader. As the system matures, the ideology takes on a radically nationalistic appearance, and the leader becomes a military ruler – a warlord. If the West were to prefer an autocratic (static) civilization for Russia, it would be choosing an inevitable recurrence of the crisis with the unavoidable consequence of aggression directed against the West itself. Each subsequent crisis would be greater than the previous one, and overcoming it would lead to the threat of an uncontrollable slide into nuclear conflict. We'd be falling into a dark historic downward spiral, where each subsequent version of Russia is worse than its predecessor.

The alternative to an autocratic, static civilization could be dynamic, federal, parliamentary stability. What I am proposing would create a dynamic political balance between a limited number of subjects of the new federation (up to twenty), with the central authorities playing the role of arbiter and director. The difference between the autocratic and the federal models for stabilization lies in the mechanism for resolving conflicts. In the autocratic model, all internal conflicts would be dealt with by the central authorities crushing, or freezing, them using political violence outside the law, and the more this is detached from society, the more effective it would be. In the federal model, on the other hand, all internal conflicts would be decided in a manageable way by a constant (dynamic) search for innumerable temporary compromises within the confines of a specially created legal and political playing field. In this instance, the central authorities could, de facto, be even stronger than in an autocracy; but this strength would be demonstrated by the authorities' control over the playing field, and not of the actual players on the field.

A shortcoming of the federal model is that it's complicated and fluid. It's a model of ongoing conflict that's built into the very foundation of the political system as part of its initial design. There's just one advantage of the federal system over the autocratic one: internal disturbances don't accumulate, but are resolved swiftly as part of the permanent struggle among the elites. As a result, there's no need for external aggression as the only possible solution for ensuring the long-term stability of the system (letting off steam). However, a rigid super-presidential republic in which the balance of power leans towards a non-executive central power is not suitable if the disagreements that regularly emerge among the elite are to be smoothly resolved and not held back for fear of repression. There would always be the temptation to return to freezing conflicts through 'unwritten rules and understandings' and stabilizing the system in the habitual way. All it would take would be for there to be one strong ruler, and then the system would inevitably slip back into the old rut. I believe that the federal system can work exclusively in the format of a parliamentary republic; in other words, as a federal parliamentary republic. The parliamentary system of government meets two requirements in the best possible way: it allows regional conflicts among the elites to be quickly resolved, and doesn't allow the system to slip easily back into the old rut.

The depth of the West's understanding of Russia's problems, and the West's position on this, will play a huge role in the success or failure of the project for a new Russia. The West must choose between an instinctive, superficial approach, and a rational, considered one. Instinctively it's easier for the West either to dream of the disintegration of Russia (giving no thought to the consequent global risks that this would bring), or to try to re-establish an autocracy with which it can have good relations (not taking into account the inevitability that these good relations would almost certainly turn sour).

The instinctive reaction is convenient because it doesn't rely on any participation on the part of the West. It gives Russia the opportunity to continue to stew in its own juice. The rational approach demands efforts from the West, similar to those that the USA took after the Second World War to shape the political process in Europe. In other words, it means the West being engaged both politically and ideologically. In this, the West must also avoid the temptation in the transitional period to split Russia up into separate parts, thus weakening the central authorities' ability to act as a political arbiter.

Turning Russia into a stable federation is a long-term historical project, and it is, above all, in the West's interests. This is not doing Russia a favour; rather, it is a rational decision, which would make the world order safer and more predictable for a significant period into the future.

20

The Legal Choice: Dictatorship of the Law or Rule-of-Law State?

If you were to conduct an opinion poll and ask passers-by on the street what they think a state governed by the rule of law is, the vast majority would answer: 'It's a state in which the law is obeyed.' This might seem to be true, but actually it's not! If things were so simple, the ideal example of a state governed by the rule of law would be the Third Reich. Whatever else you may say about it, that was a state where the laws were obeyed, and the commandant of a concentration camp who was caught taking a bribe could easily end up as an inmate, although there were cases where corrupt officials were simply transferred to other institutions. Anyway, it's not so much the observance of the law as it is the nature of the laws themselves.

A state governed by the rule of law is a state where laws are observed that meet certain criteria. What are these criteria? And why is this so important?

From time immemorial, those in power have clothed their will in the form of laws, and demanded that the population obey these laws; the people had to bow to the will of the authorities. This is the kind of archaic understanding of what is 'lawful' that still dominates in Russia. With their class approach to the law, Lenin and the Bolsheviks didn't drift far from this

archaic understanding. 'The dictatorship of the law', that they
so love to talk about in the Kremlin, is the dictatorship of the
unbridled wild will of one clan that has usurped power and has
had unchallenged control over the Kremlin for more than two
decades.

The laws whose dictatorship the Kremlin praises so highly
exist for one reason only: to give an apparent legitimacy to
naked lawlessness. These are laws of political violence. One
of the most unpleasant consequences of such a situation is
the inability of the system to adapt to any constructive evolution. Violence simply leads to more violence. And hoping that
unjust laws will, over time, develop naturally into just laws is
simply a utopian dream.

Specifically, one of the main reasons why mankind has
sought a way of escaping from unjust laws is the desire to avoid
revolution as the only way to achieve changes in society.

All those who have genuinely thought deeply about revolution have understood that it's a very difficult but unavoidable
price that society has to pay to history in order to achieve
progress. This price became unavoidable specifically because
the laws that were in operation were designed in such a way as
to prevent any change, in practice or in theory.

It's from here that the attitude has developed that revolution is a necessary evil. Loving revolution and wishing for it to
happen is as foreign to our nature as it would be to wish pain
on ourselves and those around us. (There are, of course, those
who do like this and receive pleasure from becoming involved
in the chaos of revolution.) But in a hopeless situation, the
majority of the population will see revolution simply as a lesser
evil.

If life under the old regime becomes intolerable, if all the
internal contradictions associated with this regime are brought
together in one unbreakable mess, if all the legal routes point
simply to a continuation of this lawlessness, then inevitably
thoughts turn to the sword that can cut the Gordian Knot.

This is so inevitable that it isn't worth devoting a great deal of attention to it.

A revolution happening in Russia is simply a question of when and where. A little less obvious is the question of what it will look like. But what is certainly worth considering is what measures should be taken that could help Russia in the long run to break out from its historical vicious circle, where a revolution begins after every shock. The only way to do this is to move from having unjust laws to having just laws.

There seems to be an easy answer to every question: we have to make the laws constitutional. But this only sounds simple.

First, purely formally, all the current laws appear on the surface to be in line with the Constitution. You won't find it written in the preamble of any law, even the most disgraceful, that it was passed in opposition to the letter and spirit of the Constitution.

Second, the spirit of the Constitution is something that everyone in Russia understands in their own way; and some of these ways can be rather peculiar.

Finally, only judges can have an opinion about the constitutionality of laws in Russia – and we all know who the judges are in Russia. In the overwhelming majority of cases, the unconstitutionality of laws is covered over by the practice of their implementation; but the paradox is that the practice itself long ago become a part of the law. This is indirectly confirmed by the decisions of the Constitutional Court, which is often forced to voice its opinion about laws in the specific interpretation that they're given by the practice of their implementation. So trying to change this practice without changing the laws just won't work.

So simple solutions don't work. We have to dig much deeper, until we get to those factors that make laws just, and not rely on the Constitution, which is useless for this task. Strictly speaking, there are two such factors: laws become lawful as a result of a certain procedure for their adoption, and, subsequently, because of their compliance with certain principles.

Separately, each of these conditions is insufficient. Both the procedure and the content are important here. In short, a law can be considered just if it's passed by the only legitimate legislative body: a genuine parliament that's truly independent from other branches of government and has been elected according to a democratic electoral law.

The reason for this is clear. A just law should be an expression of the consolidated will of the whole of civil society, and not just the will of a single ruler, or of a clan or class group that has seized power. It's this consolidated will that legitimizes the universally binding nature of laws and is the basis for the legitimate authorities to demand its strict observance by all.

Parliament is the melting pot in which the political will of civil society is transformed into the texts of laws.

If we look more closely at the work of a parliament, we see that, as well as the consolidation of the political will of various segments of civil society, each of which has its own specific interests, it also has another function. On any question that's become a topic of discussion in society, parliament brings together the simple view with the learned – expert – view.

This is why it's so important that a parliament be independent both from the executive and from the society that's elected it (just for the period of its term and not, of course, permanently).

In parliament, the political will of the ordinary voter is passed through the sieve of expert analysis. And the other way round: the opinions of experts are subjected to the scrutiny of the highest political appraisal.

It is vital to maintain this balance. What we've seen in recent years is that the expert opinion imposed by the government from above has overruled the view of civil society. As a result, laws have simply stopped operating, or are just not accepted by society.

Incidentally, the dictatorship of society would lead to the same result, but from the opposite side: this would lead to the practical impossibility of fulfilling 'political wish lists'.

The procedure for passing just laws is extremely complicated, which is why it's so important. There are a great many minute details involved in it, many of which seem to be mere formalities; yet none of them can be neglected. This system has built up over centuries, even thousands of years, and has absorbed international political experience. And despite this, it's unique to every culture and to every specific historic situation.

Russia will have to carefully comprehend and master this experience of parliamentary government, not so as to blindly imitate or simplify it, but in order to develop the only suitable system on the basis of this experience. When it operates normally it will allow for the adoption of just laws.

It's essential to add that even the best format cannot alter the need for the correct content. Even the most perfect parliament, which represents the consolidated political will of civil society and where there's a perfect balance of social and expert opinion, cannot guarantee that its laws will be just (although without the parliament they certainly won't be). These laws must meet certain criteria; that is, they should be built on certain principles that exist neither in time nor in space.

These principles are, in a way, political axioms that are accepted a priori by society in a liberal democracy; that is, on faith.

Paradoxically, it doesn't matter whether they're written into the Constitution, cast in granite, or exist merely in the minds of citizens. There are countries that don't have a written constitution but in which these principles are strictly adhered to. There are yet other countries that have detailed constitutions and principles in writing for every eventuality of life – yet none of them is kept. What matters is not what's written or where it's written, but how firmly it's taken hold in people's minds.

In my view, one of these basic principles is the idea of freedom. This isn't surprising. After all, in its own way the law is a measure of freedom. This concept of the law developed as a result of the marriage between the traditions of Western Antiquity (from the Greeks and the Romans) and those of Christianity. We can extend this to say that herein lies the basis of Europeanism and the modern age.

If we consider our ability to accept such a concept of the law and of just laws, we can judge whether Russia is ready to be a European country. All other indicators are far less relevant or indicative.

In order to understand whether a particular law is just or not, it must be examined under this political microscope. And whatever formal relationship or coincidence of language there may be with any other law, this is not proof of whether or not a law is correct. It's especially important to stress this, bearing in mind the Kremlin's habit of pointing to international practice and covering up its lawlessness by the decisions of the Constitutional Court, which it has made impotent.

Indeed, laws are passed about public gatherings, about extremism, about showing disrespect to the authorities or about mass unrest, on pre-trial agreements with the investigators, on streamlining proceedings in criminal cases, and so forth. We constantly hear how, in Russia, everything's exactly the same as it is 'over there' in other countries – and even a lot better.

Yes, if we're talking about the wording of the laws, then we have a lot in common. But here's the rub: the very same words work differently in different political situations and produce different results. This proves just one thing: comparing the words of laws doesn't work. We have to look more closely at the details.

In each and every case, we have to consider the actual economic and sociopolitical situation, and ask whether a particular law protects the rights and freedoms of the individual.

And it's not as easy to do this as many seem to think. The principle of freedom is often contrary to other principles and values that are guaranteed by the Constitution. For example, freedom to hold demonstrations and freedom of assembly clearly restrict the rights of those who have no intention of demonstrating or assembling and who just want to have a quiet and tasty meal in a café on the same boulevard. This is a genuine contradiction. So what can we do?

We could decide in favour of those who are taking part in the demonstration, who are clearly in the minority; or we could rule in favour of those who want to relax in a normal manner; they're clearly the majority. Naturally, the Russian authorities resolve this contradiction to their own advantage, but by hiding behind the majority, who always want to eat. Thus the laws on public gatherings in Russia are seemingly just like those in Europe; but in reality they operate in the mythical land of Asiopa [a disparaging 'backwards' term for the interior portion of Eurasia, i.e. the former USSR – Ed.].

This is because a conflict shouldn't be decided in favour simply of the majority or the minority, but in favour of freedom as a stand-alone value. In this particular case, the question should be decided in such a way that priority protection is given to freedom of political action.

Only a law that has this as its basis can be considered just.

It's interesting to note that in the years since Putin's been in power, Russia has distanced itself one hundred per cent from Europe and has moved closer to Asiopa. Some adherents of the dictatorship of the law have even gone so far as to propose revising the hierarchy of the branches of legislation that has been generally accepted since Soviet times, arguing that criminal law should stand at the top of the pyramid, not constitutional law. This, of course, is another loyalist stupidity, but at the same time it is very indicative.

These are the people who say 'the law' and mean 'autocracy'.

And when they talk about 'autocracy' they have in mind 'the law'.

Why have I spent so much time on this apparently tangential and deeply philosophical question? Because I believe it's fundamental. There are certain things that you don't need to prove to anyone. Among those who are opposed to the regime there is agreement that the current law-enforcement and judicial system are anti-constitutional and in need of deep revolutionary transformation. There have been many suggestions as to how this could be done, most of which make sense and are very useful.

Multi-page, fundamental reports and serious and voluminous academic papers, as well as brilliant short essays, have been written that are full of specific suggestions and complete reform projects. The general outlines are clear. The competence of jury trials should be expanded and the independence of the courts strengthened; the FSB should be transformed from a 'second government' into a body focused on combating terrorism and espionage; in general, the special services should be downsized and diversified; there should be a radical change in the role of the prosecutor's office; and much more besides. But none of these suggestions will be of any use unless the main revolution takes place: inside people's heads. Nothing will change if people don't understand the essence of what the concept of just laws really means.

Any structure can be cut short, any mechanism can be perverted, any guarantee can be circumvented if there's no agreement on the main principle: the criterion by which the success or failure of reforms is judged. And here there is just one criterion: freedom. It is the priority of freedom that overturns the unjust law and adopts the just law; and that overturns the dictatorship of the law, that's dangerous for society (and acts merely as a fig leaf for a new autocracy) and ensures that the state is governed by the rule of law.

21

The Moral Choice: Justice or Mercy?

Max Weber once noted that if you scratch the most rational theory, you'll find that it's based on some totally irrational idea that we accept on faith. This idea is what's holding together everything that we regard as completely rational and logical.

It's also the case that, at the root of any political programme, is some kind of moral imperative, which we vote for not with our minds but with our hearts. This voting with the heart is more important than voting using your intellect. In most cases, logical mistakes can be corrected; but moral errors are usually fatal.

It's generally accepted that the fundamental moral imperative in politics is justice. Society reacts angrily to any violation of the balance of justice, and if the pendulum swings too far then it restores this balance by means of a revolution. Yet if you ask the average person what the essence of justice is, very few can give you an answer. However, ask someone whether they think that Russia is today run 'justly', then the vast majority – including many supporters of the regime – will answer with a categorical 'no'.

In a nutshell, this is the regime's main problem. On the

moral level, it's rejected by the majority of its habitual political 'fan base'. The restoration of justice can be delayed, but it can't be avoided. Sooner or later, this secret political lever will get pulled and will turn over the next page of history.

You'd think that there would be nothing simpler then bringing morality back into politics: all you have to do is restore justice. But when you look closely at justice, nothing is as simple as it might have seemed.

First of all, each person has their own idea of what justice means, and it's very difficult to find a definition that everyone would agree on. Second, and more importantly, the price of restoring the balance of justice can often be staggeringly high. We must never forget that the Bolshevik Revolution took place on the crest of a wave of a search by the Russian people for justice, and its sworn aim was specifically the creation of the most just society in the world. But it ended up as an even more unjust society, which dragged on for decades.

So the search for justice must itself be done in a balanced way. We have to find a balance for the balance, so as not to turn history into an hourglass, using a revolution to turn it over from time to time. Whenever our intention is to 'knock down the world of violence to its foundations, then build our new world', we are simply – like in the joke quoted earlier – 'making our own Kalashnikov rifle', which we use over and over again to destroy both Russian civil society and the green shoots of a state governed by the rule of law.

So that we don't repeat this, we must put haphazard searches for justice inside a framework. I think that this framework can be constructed in only one way: by basing it on a moral principle that's even deeper and more universal than justice.

For me, this principle is mercy.

Mercy is the ability to empathize and to forgive; it's the second level of justice. If we measure politics and the law by justice, then we use mercy to measure justice itself, by not allowing it to turn into its opposite.

The irony of history is that every promise to build a more just world usually ends up with the building of a 'just' concentration camp. Justice for some quickly turns dialectically into harsh injustice for others. Each time, the restoration of justice becomes an expensive project, and those seeking it end up paying for it, as do subsequent generations.

If we want to avoid repeating this same story, we have to acknowledge that naked justice and naked truth are never as attractive as we might wish them to be. It's only when we rely on mercy that we have the opportunity to turn our clever solutions into wise ones. These may seem to be mere words. They are not. They are an attempt to put forward an alternative point of reference for considering and solving the most important practical questions of our political life.

What direct and indirect consequences could there be for the discussion on Russia's future if we place justice, supported by mercy, at the forefront? There are quite a few.

First, the clear division between 'us' and 'them' disappears. 'We' are the holy ones, 'they' are the fiends from hell. If we understand not only ourselves but others, too, we cannot draw such a line.

We have all, to some extent or another, been responsible for what has happened 'with our Motherland and with ourselves'. Some because they took part, others because they failed to take part. No one is completely right, and no one is completely guilty. There is no 'Great Wall' in the issue of responsibility between the beneficiaries of the regime and its victims.

From the point of view of revolutionary justice, there are two camps: we've been made to suffer, now it's your turn. From the point of view of mercy, there is one society, one nation, one people. Yes, they're sick. They're suffering from low morale and cultural decline. But to a greater or lesser degree this affects everyone. There are very few nowadays who can put themselves in the position of being the one without sin who can cast the first stone.

Second – and this follows on from the first point – before we can demand change from others we have to be prepared to change ourselves. Each of us has inside us some poison that we have to squeeze out.

If society's energy is focused solely on searching for and punishing 'the guilty', while we ourselves remain unchanged, then nothing good will come out of this battle for justice. It's only if we're prepared to be more honest with ourselves and more tolerant towards those who are different from us that we can avoid falling into yet another social extreme, simply replacing one lot of satraps and thieves with another lot.

A third point, developing this idea further, is that history shows that forgiveness can sometimes be cheaper than punishment. If given free rein, the natural and just desire for revenge turns into an all-engulfing fire, destroying not only those on whom we seek revenge, but ourselves, too. Revenge, including social and political revenge, should never become the dominant idea in society, its all-consuming passion. If it does, you will never escape trouble. When we're blaming and scourging the regime, which is considered an essential element of cleaning it out, we must nevertheless remember that forgiveness is more important than punishment, and that everyone has the right to repentance. You'll never build a new society on bitterness and revenge.

Fourthly, we have to distinguish between the 'first disciples' and those who 'lived like everyone else'. Their roles have not been identical, and thus their fates should be different. For a quarter of a century, a corrupting, amoral matrix has been developing in society's behaviour. In this matrix, good and evil, black and white, have swapped places. Tens of millions of people were drawn into this matrix and lived according to its unwritten rules. Many of them were totally unaware that they were participating in the crimes of the regime; many were aware, but were not acting on their own initiative.

But there were also the 'first disciples', those who created and nurtured this matrix: they corrupted the nation, developed the mafia state, and became its main beneficiaries. There should be a different approach to them.

Finally, we must realize once and for all that, although remaking society is harder than shooting those responsible, remaking is precisely what we must do, convincing people to live differently and play by the new rules.

We can't bring down from the moon a different race and swap those we have for 'ideal citizens'. Nearly all our government officials are corrupt, not because they were born to be such monsters, but because, in the matrix that developed, there was no other way to operate. If you didn't steal, you wouldn't survive. And we can't simply sack all government officials in one day. The ranks of those who could do their work are very thin. If anyone were to try to go down this route, the country would become ungovernable in an instant.

Incidentally, Lenin understood this very quickly, when within eighteen months Communist Russia collapsed into ruin and starvation. Even if we were able to sack all the officials and put in their places new and fresh people, we would very quickly see that the new ones would rob the people even more than did our former 'masters of the universe'. We've seen this in Russia more than once. Our task has to be not to sack and ostracize, but to make people work in a different way. And that's much more difficult.

This all encourages me to give my thoughts on two of the most important topics of public discussion in recent years: lustration and revolution.

Lustration. There is a partially justified view that the compromises of the revolution carried out by Mikhail Gorbachev and Boris Yeltsin, especially as regards the ban on the activities of the Communist Party and the lustration of members of the KGB, played a significant role in the history of post-Communist Russia and led us to where we are today. This seems entirely plausible, considering the role that former members of the KGB played at the start of the twenty-first century in decisively restoring the Soviet regime, and the opportunistic role that the self-appointed heirs of the Communist Party are playing today, rolling back the years to 'orthodox Stalinism' and the 'populism of the Black Hundreds'.

Is there a lesson to be learnt from this for the future? When the regime collapses (and sooner or later it will collapse; it's just a question of time), should we wield a sword and punish everyone who works in the security services, all judges, all prosecutors, and so on? Should we finally ban the Communists, and at the same time remove the right to work in government service from members of United Russia, A Just Russia, followers of the Liberal Democratic Party of Russia, and the activists of the All-Russian National Front?

It looks tempting. But maybe a warning sign is that when they did something similar in Ukraine and Georgia it didn't really help.

For the reasons given above ('you can't shoot them all'), there'd be no one left to do the work; there's no guarantee that those who take their places would be considerably better; and many of those who work in the security structures these days carry out their duties honestly and, at great risk to their lives, fight against terrorism and criminals.

It's true that our judges are all defiled and corrupted by lawlessness. But perhaps it's not so much the fault of the judges as of those who've defiled them? If we remove the Kremlin gang, if we conduct a serious inquiry, if we give professional people the chance to be both people and professionals . . .

No, of course it's much better to start afresh, with a new page; but where are we going to find this new page? And besides, you can't treat millions of our fellow citizens as if they were nothing more than dust – of course, you could just wipe them away, and lo! There's Stalin's pockmarked mug staring back at you from the mirror . . .

I'm against lustration across the board. It's never really been completely successful anywhere. The Bolsheviks went further with this than anyone else. They effectively completed the process of lustration using the meat-grinder of the Great Terror in 1937, but they still didn't achieve what they'd set out to do.

As a rule, approaching everything based on one and the same template rarely produces a good result. Of course, we have to conduct a thorough and large-scale investigation of the crimes of the regime and identify the key beneficiaries of the mafia state, the real culprits of the escalation of repression and lawlessness. These people must be judged and punished under an open and public due process of law (with all legal guarantees being observed; those very guarantees that they denied others), even if society then decides to grant them amnesty.

As for those who are less responsible for what the regime has done, they can be dealt with using 'nominal measures'.

A different matter is 'institutional lustration', which should be carried out as strictly and consistently as possible. The point is not that KGB officers weren't removed, but that eventually this same KGB itself was restored as a universal repressive institution that carried out the role of a second (sometimes the first) government. Such lustration is not a witch hunt, but a ruthless thinning out of a dense forest that turns people into witches and goblins.

Things usually happen the other way round with us. In the battle for justice, we seem ready to shoot the evil creatures, but not touch the game reserve where they lived and bred. The solution, which has to be real, long term and not just temporary, is not in settling scores, or in lustration and purges, but in profound institutional reforms. We won't get by without purges, but they should be tempered by mercy, which will lessen the desire to seek revenge.

Revolution. Everything is leading to the idea that yet another revolution in Russia is inevitable. The regime is stuck in a rut of repression, from which it wouldn't be easy to extract itself even if it wanted to; and it has no desire to do this. It has just one desire: to hold on to power at any price. The key word here is 'any'. This sense of an impending revolution is gradually creeping into every layer of society, affecting even those who are loyal to the regime and are benefiting quite nicely from it. What can we say about those who've chosen the path of professional revolutionaries?

The authorities have done so much to turn revolution into a scarecrow that they're now reaping the opposite reaction. For many people, a revolution – and the bigger, the better – appears to be the most desirable and most positive solution to the growing crisis.

Is revolution as good as our imagination makes it out to be? Far from it. A revolution always has its very dark, hidden side. It is counterintuitive for a person to want a revolution, because it'll be a huge shock for the whole of society. But it's too late to think of that now. Now, it's as necessary as a scalpel is to a surgeon. Understanding and accepting the historical necessity we face, and with a past experience that is shared by very few nations of the world, we nonetheless have to do everything in our power to ensure that the revolution does not become the end in itself. We mustn't put an end to lawlessness and violence by setting up a festival of violence and lawlessness.

Revolutions cost society too much for them to become instruments for settling scores or reallocating resources. While admiring the revolutions that have taken place in the post-Soviet space, we must remember that their medium-term results turned out to be far removed from the expectations of those who inspired and created them.

We must never lose sight of the main aim of the revolution: to make society more humane, more tolerant and more free. As well as the political and economic results it brings, the revolution should usher in added moral value, which is why it can't just be handed over to the cynics and political strategists.

The revolution can belong to the whole population, which, having experienced it, will then be morally cleansed and freed. Despite the cost, such a revolution is good for society. Or, alternatively, the revolution can belong to a revolutionary party, which carries it out in the name of the people but actually in its own interests. Such a revolution is worthless – except for the party functionaries.

A revolution isn't needed to destroy the old order. You don't need to be very clever to do that. A revolution is needed in order to build something new in place of the old order, something based on equal measures of justice and mercy.

If such a new order doesn't arise out of this, then the revolution will have failed. Today, in the heat of the struggle, we're often too focused on the negative side of the revolution, on the need to demolish a regime that's hated by many. This is understandable, especially now that this regime has switched to a policy of open mass repression. But if we fail to switch the centre of gravity to the positive side of the revolution, to our ideals, to our dreams about a society and state based on the rule of law, then we will devalue any victory over the regime and end up even further away from our goal than we were before.

The passion of the fight, the desire to take revenge, the desire to see the monsters at least nailed to a pillory: all these are understandable and largely justified. All by itself this regime has provoked in its opponents feelings of hatred and rejection. But if, as we look into the future, we're ruled by these emotions alone, then we won't go far. Ultimately, the winner will be the one who can rise above these emotions and give everyone the chance to take part in creating a new, open Russia.

22

Victory for Ukraine: An End or a Beginning?

About What Kind of Peace We Need, and What Kind We Should Try to Avoid

M uch has been written in this book about Russia's war against Ukraine, about aggression, about what would constitute a fair and just peace and why we should settle for nothing less. I'll now briefly summarize what I've already said so far.

War is the very essence of the system that Putin has created. Right now, there is a lot of ongoing discussion about the question of when exactly it was that war became inevitable. The only correct answer is: 'At the moment Putin came to power.' War is built into the philosophy of the regime he has created. Or, more precisely, into its reliance on violence and corruption as all-purpose tools for running a state. This means either the rule of law and a civil society (peace) or violence, corruption and, as a result, war. Putin now faces a choice between a civil war and an imperialist war – which is, in essence, just taking the civil war beyond the confines of the national borders. Having chosen violence over the rule of law for Russia, Putin has thereby made war inevitable. He began his leadership with war (the Second Chechen War of 1999), and with war he will end it (be it the Second Ukrainian War or the First Baltic/Balkan/Polish War). Which one it will be depends on the stoutness of the Ukrainian armed forces and the resolve of the West.

No sustainable peace deal with Putin is possible without changing the system he has created. There are no conditions out there that would 'satisfy' Putin. And this is not because his thirst for money and territories is insatiable (although the idea of going down in history as 'the gatherer of the Russian lands' does warm the cockles of his heart), but because in fact he goes to war with one, and only one, objective – to squeeze at least some benefit for himself from the protests against his irremovability, ultra-centralization and corruption. Any lull in the fighting will lead to an increase in protests, which will only force him once again to undertake ever bigger military adventures, spreading the virus of aggression to new territories.

Compromises with Putin simply serve to reinforce his belief that aggression is an all-purpose way of resolving any conflicts, be they external or internal. It isn't about the territories that Russia has annexed as such. It's about the fact that recognizing Putin's right to any 'trophies' in this war is a direct path to the next war.

In this chapter I want to focus my attention on something else; something about which, for understandable reasons, little has been said or written so far, because there has been no time yet to think about it. I want to write about what the future world will look like. Along with everybody else, I don't know how this war is going to end. I can make guesses, but I can't know for sure. But there is one thing that I do know for certain: it will end at some point and, when it does, there will still be a Ukraine and a Russia, no matter what other ideas some people might have. And this means that there is going to be some kind of relationship between the two of them, certainly not friendly, but somewhere in the broad range from extremely hostile to coolly neutral. I think that the time has already come when we need to start thinking about just what kind of peace we would like to see between Ukraine and Russia. Of all the possible realistic scenarios, which one should we be aiming for?

Stripping away any extraneous details, we end up with two basic scenarios for how the post-war world might look: the Israeli-Palestinian model and the Franco-German one. In both of these, the conflict started out being existential in nature; that is, the war was being waged with the objective of complete and total annihilation of the other side and of its statehood. In both cases, the hot phase of the war ended at some point, but in different ways. Between the Israelis and the Palestinians, a temporary truce was established under pressure from international sponsors for whom further support of this war had become too heavy a burden. In the Franco-German case, the conflict ended with the total defeat of one side (Germany) and the resolution of a historical territorial dispute in favour of the other side (France).

Despite the fact that the outcome of the war between France and Germany appears to be more uncompromising, we should note that, at the end of the day, after many decades, a strong and lasting alliance was created between them, while the war itself remained nothing more than a dark page in their historical memory. On the contrary, in the dispute between Israel and Palestine, where too much was left open-ended in the negotiated truce, the situation is only getting worse and armed clashes erupt practically every day, each time threatening to boil over into a new war.

The first lesson that we can take away from these two very different experiences is that compromises are not always useful in the long term and that calls for a cessation of hostilities at any cost may lead not to peace, but to a military dead-end. For this reason, it makes more sense strategically to try to achieve a peace based on principled conditions – that is, for it to be a just peace and not any old peace made simply for its own sake. We need to be thinking about this when we hear calls for an immediate unconditional stop to the war.

But this isn't the only proviso. There is yet another one, and one that's far more important to my mind: namely, that relations are established in a pragmatic way, based on the principle of rational egoism. This may sound strange, but that doesn't make it any the less important. The essence of the problem is that everything will depend on what motives guide both the leaders of the currently warring countries and, above all, the cultural elites (for it is they who, at the end of the day, will define the overall long-term conditions) once (and if) the desired just peace is reached (which in my opinion means the full and proper punishment of the aggressor and the aggression). There are two options here: the motive of *ressentiment* (or hostile resentment) and the motive of advantage. The second motive may seem basic and cynical, but unfortunately this is the only one that can ultimately pull us out of the pit in which the war has buried us.

In my opinion, the essence of a *ressentiment* policy was best expressed by Golda Meir when she said that opponents of the Israeli state were making fatal mistakes because their actions were being guided not by what was advantageous for them, but by making sure that nothing was done that might be advantageous for Israel. I think this is the key here. If, after the war, the two sides continue to be guided by the principle of 'anything at all, as long as it hurts the other guys more than it hurts us', then there will never be a firm and lasting peace. We must do whatever it takes to get out of the trap of a zero-sum game mentality and find a path to peace that is built on the basis of the rules of cooperative games.

But what does this mean in practice? First of all, we need to accept as a given that neither Ukraine nor Russia is going to disappear from the map; they are going to have to coexist as neighbours, sharing a huge land border and complex connections on many levels, including human family ties as well as economic, social and other relations. This, by the way, will be no easy task, because today the emotional intensity of the Ukrainian population is the polar opposite of that of the Russian population. At the level of propaganda, which shapes the mass consciousness, the dominant premise is that one of the main objectives of this war is annihilation of the adversary (the disintegration of Russia or of Ukraine, depending on which side you're on). Overcoming this paradigm, acknowledging and understanding that the priority is instead to find peaceful coexistence, would be an important step towards achieving a long-term peace. But in fact, trade is the engine that makes the world go round, and neighbourly trading relations are more effective than kinship and friendship.

What can really help facilitate the normalization of relations is a lack of fear. As experience has shown, weakness is an impetus and motive for aggression. In connection with this, I believe that, whenever this war ends, its result must include real and robust guarantees to Ukraine on the part of NATO (whether this involves Ukraine actually joining NATO is unimportant), and not the kind of assurances contained in the 1994 Budapest Memorandum. At the risk of repeating myself, this is, above all, in Russia's interests. And, of course, in Ukraine's as well. Because only if Ukraine and the Ukrainian people believe that they are reliably defended against any recidivist aggression can relations between them and Russia have a chance of slowly stabilizing.

Last, but certainly not least, it would not be right to try to rush any processes, even those that to some might seem positive. After all that has happened, a historical pause to take breath is necessary and beneficial from both the human and the political perspective. There is no need to try to lock each other into an embrace right away. We just need to give people time to come round again, and for this we need first to give them a chance to create a little space between themselves. For some period of time, a bit of distancing – including emotional, cultural and business – is healthy and healing. Time and distance are the best doctors following a war. And, if we allow them to work, then, maybe later, for subsequent generations, a window of opportunity will open up for some kind of rapprochement.

Conclusion:
The Dragon in Custody

The dragon has gone too far in its war against the people, and, as a result, all its heads, however many there are, should remember that they carry personal responsibility for what is happening and that it's already too late to set the tab back to zero. At the same time, I wish to address myself to those who entered the Russian Colosseum to watch the battle against the dragon, hoping to applaud the heroes from the safety of the stands. When I was sitting in my prison cell, I used to read your articles praising the heroes, and I still read them today. I see in them the desire that someone will slay the dragon for you. I see a terrible disappointment when this doesn't happen.

I became interested enough to ask: do you understand that, should your wish come true and someone slays the dragon for you, your disappointment will be even greater?

In order to become a professional dragon-slayer, a person must themselves either be a dragon at the outset, or else become a dragon in the process. And then their team will be a typical dragon's team, with the same methods and aims.

And if you think that the hero will fight the dragon and that you'll receive the benefits (freedom and democracy, at least), then you're naive (if, that is, you really are expecting to receive freedom and democracy, and not simply work as a servant). We already went through this with Boris Yeltsin.

Can the dragon be slain? Of course it can. That's not the issue. The main question is: why do it? And it's much more difficult to answer that than many people realize.

For me and for many of my fellow citizens, the unbroken thousand-year history of Russia is important. The roots of our common European – and now our Euro-Atlantic – civilization are important.

It's important for me that we're not aliens in this Western world, but among its creators and defenders. Yes, we lost a great deal when we protected Western civilization from the Tatar-Mongol horde, from the Asian invasion, and, as a result, we became different people; but in our culture we didn't become Asian. I don't want to say anything against the ancient and wonderful Asian culture, just that it's not ours. We're closer to William Shakespeare and Miguel de Cervantes than we are to Hafez Shirazi or Sun Tzu.

The modern world isn't simply globalization, communication and cooperation. It's also competition on a new, global level, on the level of world civilizations.

Endless wars and contempt for human life have left us with far too little to suggest that we could afford to start another, new, separate, yet competitive civilization.

Of course, there's always a place on the fringes of progress, and the modern world is sufficiently humane and prudent not to encroach upon this fringe. There are gentle ways to use those who are too weak to take part in real competition.

But I hate the idea that my country might occupy this space! We are Europeans! We helped build and defend this civilization and have as much right to our place in it as do the French, the Germans, the British, the Australians, the Canadians or the Americans!

For centuries we've walked side by side, shoulder to shoulder with them, and we know that we need them all and they need us. We refuse to listen to stupid and greedy people who want to drive us apart for their own selfish ends.

Yes, we can find a lot of events in history that it would have been better had they not happened, but even our troubles and our wars have been shared. To this day, we remember the 50 million people who died in Europe in just the Second World War alone, both friends and enemies. But the 50 million who died in China – what do we know about them? Do you feel the difference?

The first working title of this book was *Gardarika: The Country of Cities*. Why? Because Gardarika was a country from those long-off times when Europe was one. And we will be that again; it's our historic destiny. But having our place at the shared table depends on us. It depends on our talent, our brains, our ability to anticipate the future and achieve those specific goals that will make us, our children and our grand-children happy.

I'm making my contribution to this work. May whoever is capable of it do more – and better.